A Living Tradition

CAC Publishing

Center *for* Action *and* Contemplation

CAC.ORG

"Oneing" is an old English word that was used by Lady Julian of Norwich (1342–1416) to describe the encounter between God and the soul. The Center for Action and Contemplation proudly borrows the word to express the divine unity that stands behind all of the divisions, dichotomies, and dualisms in the world. We pray and publish with Jesus's words, "that all may be one" (John 17:21).

editor:
Mark Longhurst

associate editor:
Shirin McArthur

editorial consultant:
Stephen Copeland

publisher:
The Center for Action and Contemplation

advisory board:
David Benner
James Danaher
Ilia Delio, OSF
Sheryl Fullerton
Stephen Gaertner, OPraem

Layout by Taylor Sampson and artwork by Izzy Spitz

oneing

VOLUME 13 NO. 2

Editor's Note

MY ROOTS IN CHRISTIANITY go back to the serious and often uptight folks called Congregationalists who trace themselves to the New England Puritans. I wasn't taught about a wider, big "T" Tradition of mystics, prophets, and saints who dedicated their lives to exemplifying and drinking from the well of divine love. As a young clergyperson still questioning my beliefs, I stumbled into the living Tradition of contemplative Christianity via Richard Rohr and the CAC. In my late twenties, I drove windy and wooded roads from Massachusetts to Connecticut to attend a retreat with Fr. Richard and two hundred others on the true and false selves. I heard for the first time that the divine presence in me participates in the divine presence that knits together reality. Tasting silence for the first time, I gulped from the Spirit's nourishing waters of contemplative Christianity like a thirsty desert wanderer happening upon a hidden oasis.

The articles in this issue of *Oneing* point the way toward living water for thirsty wanderers. They illuminate a path of transformation and depth that has been present in the Christian tradition all along, even if it remained a hidden and best-kept secret. As Fr. Adam Bucko puts it, this path is the Christian tradition: "Contemplation is not a fringe part of Christianity. It is Christianity—lived deeply." Engaged, contemplative Christianity is the dynamic, evolving, living movement of God unfolding in history—and in our own lives and time.

This special issue of *Oneing* is a celebration, dialogue with, and exploration of this living Tradition. Richard Rohr reminds us that the liberating message of Jesus is a central reference point, continued in the teaching and witness of a Franciscan "alternative orthodoxy." Rachel Wheeler invites us to discover the "desert magic" of "resistance, refuge, and revelation" conjured by the desert fathers and mothers in the early centuries of Christianity. Katie Gordon looks to her experience in Benedictine monasticism to show us that at heart, the monk is "someone who teaches us about ongoing renewal." E. Trey Clark points to Black contemplative preachers in more recent times such as Sojourner Truth and Howard Thurman as those who "pursued the flourishing of Black people" while offering guidance into our shared experience of God.

Careful attention to mystical texts, such as that paid by translator Carmen Acevedo Butcher, becomes a mutual dialogue that does not leave us unchanged. Reading the living tradition, including even the words of this issue, is an invitation to communion with reality's merciful embrace. Cassidy Hall looks to the inspiration of Thomas Merton for encouragement that even though we do not know where we are going, we know that we are not alone. Through mystical poets of darkness like Hadewijch, Douglas Christie affirms that in the unknowing, a powerful love still beckons us.

This living tradition lures us further into—not away from—reality. Authentic spirituality does not bypass anything. It instead compels us to "keep our hearts open in hell," as Mirabai Starr dares. Christine Valters Paintner observes that illness itself becomes a threshold of possible inner change. Contemporary tools such as the Twelve Steps offer a mystical itinerary, as Kris Vieira Coleman charts. The psychological wisdom that integrates our "shadow" selves, Elise Loehnen writes, gives us the "space and grace in allowing ourselves to be whole."

But for this living tradition to breathe, it must not only be for us. Dr. Barbara Holmes, in an adapted talk from one of the CAC's CONSPIRE conferences, reminds us that contemplation can catch us when, in the shared crisis of oppression, "we are in freefall toward the center of our being." The gift of divine compassion never turns in on itself, but stands in loving witness with others who suffer, as exemplified in Alison McCrary's work with death-row inmates. Drew Jackson prays that silence may be a bridge to love, even amid the shattered rubble of the violence we inflict upon one another. Ultimately, engaged contemplative Christianity, as Brian McLaren tells us, has a critical role to play "in times of emergency and unraveling, collaborat[ing] broadly in the 'great turning' upon which our future depends." May it be so.

Mark Longhurst

Editor, Oneing

Desert
Magic

By Rachel Wheeler

T HE DESERT OCCUPIES a powerful place at the heart of Jewish, Christian, and Islamic spiritual traditions. Simultaneously, the desert is a place of resistance, refuge, and revelation. In the early centuries of Christianity, the desert was home for those seeking countercultural withdrawal. Many men and women, who came to be known as desert fathers and mothers, experienced the wilderness as a refuge from an Empire increasingly inhospitable to them.

Why did they experience Empire as inhospitable? For one reason, the Roman Empire was a site of injustice and conflict: between men and women, lower and upper classes, political insiders and outsiders, ethnic majorities and minorities. For another, Christianity was seen by many as having been coopted by Empire when it became the official state religion. As such, its association with the powerful and wealthy was inconsistent with how many desert mothers and fathers believed they ought to live out their Christian calling.

The ways these desert Christians navigated the difficulties of their own time and place may seem irredeemably remote to most of us, but I find their stories strangely compelling, like stones yielding different veins of mineral and precious metals whichever way you turn them. Their stories and teachings are brief, sometimes cryptic, sometimes profound, as these gruff desert patriots rubbed shoulders with each other and uncovered uncomfortable knowledge of themselves and their habits of thought, fallibilities, and limitations.

I identify with these desert Christians in their gruffness, slow willingness to accept change, and reluctant curiosity about what's possible. Even more, I identify with their friends and visitors who marveled at them and collected their words for us to ponder centuries later. In these collections, I sense particular kinds of magic: the desert's maternal magic, the magic that happens with freedom from possession, and the magic of love disguised as deception.

THE MATERNAL DESERT

OR THE FIFTH-CENTURY WRITER Eucherius of Lyon (c. 380–c. 449), the desert was the "mother's lap."[1] Another source speaks of the desert as offering up children to God, formed as good spiritual beings by the desert's maternal care.[2] The desert could be a place of safety and nourishment, despite the privations many experienced living off-grid, as it were. It was hard work for desert Christians to build themselves dwellings, to find adequate and sustainable sources of food and water, and to endure an onslaught of tempting thoughts and regrets with the potential to undermine their commitment to a contemplative life of recognizing and responding to God's presence.

What to make of this feminine image in literature so lacking in attention to women's lives? This redirection of attention from the physical companionship of human women to a feminization of the landscape is important.

To experience the desert as loving mother opened a way to understand themselves as gratuitously gifted with life, even amid what appeared difficult.

It reminds us that it's impossible to do *without* the feminine, however much these male solitaries tried. The need and desire for the feminine persisted and even radically extended to comprise the entire landscape, from its suppression within and among themselves. To experience the desert as loving mother opened a way to understand themselves as gratuitously gifted with life, even amid what appeared difficult.

The desert offered a particular kind of formation. It could be harsh, offering unwelcome discipline as a parent might. It required the desert dwellers to grow up and fend for themselves, to play well with others, and to share—all guidance we may have received from our own parents at one time! The desert would have offered a strange kind of consolation, as well, when loneliness or the particular boredom called *acedia* kicked in. Wild animals might have offered companionship, as they did for Abba Theon, who made his solitary home in the desert, sharing food and water with the wild animals who visited his dwelling.[3]

The prototypical desert father, Antony of Egypt (251–356), is said to have *fallen in love* with the place he lived, deep in the desert, where a few palm trees, water, and arable soil made an oasis.[4] This was the desert's magic: that within what appeared scarce, there might emerge surprising abundance. What could be harsh might offer a warm welcome. The landscape's paradox offered space for theological paradox: The incarnation! The virgin birth! The Trinity! The Apostle Paul's simultaneous willing and not-willing to do good! Even: the subtle interplay of the body's, mind's, and spirit's needs! The desert helped these Christians lean more deeply into undermining their assumptions and cravings for what is and what should be.

THE PARADOXICAL NATURE OF
NON-POSSESSIVE LOVE

MY FAVORITE STORIES about the desert Christians are contained in collections arranged alphabetically by a person's name or thematically by a desired virtue (or vice to avoid). In the alphabetical collections, we may note with disappointment that only three women are named in contrast to over one hundred names of men. Alas, the patriarchy of Christianity has deep roots, even as resistance to that cultural norm was part of the project of the desert. Many women seem to have experienced the liberative magic of a desert life, allowing them to move beyond scripted roles of wife and mother. That this liberty often required echoing men's ways of being makes me wonder what might have been if women's ways of being were more directly celebrated in the tradition.

In the thematic collections of stories about desert Christians, a chapter on Love (*agape*) points us to what these early Christians considered to be the way they should treat one another and outsiders. These are poignant stories that brush up harshly against our own values and behaviors and remind us why these stories still seem alive and potent, despite nearly two thousand years' distance from us.

One of these stories tells of two friends living together who took it into their heads to take a break from their countercultural life and live like others.[5] To do this, they seemed to think they needed to engineer a situation in which they had to contend with each other over possessions. That this seemed the best way to embody a typical encounter tells us a lot about their culture (and our own)! So, these two friends set a brick between them and proceeded to argue about whose brick it was. This couldn't last long. Almost immediately, they became fatigued by the process, so that one of them simply took the other's "It's mine!" for real and shrugged off the attempt to fight. Off they went, the story ends in a short paragraph, not having found anything to quarrel about. These friends had achieved a kind of relationship in which ownership and contention over possessions made absolutely no sense. They could not keep up the pretense that such things mattered in the life they were trying to live in the desert.

Another story tells of a desert Christian who removed the basket handles from his own woven wares to give to another desert dweller who wanted them for his own. The sacrifice emerges, curiously, as a deception, because the generous desert Christian claims the handles were *left over* from his own construction of baskets rather than removed from his own finished goods. The short story, again only a paragraph in length, ends: "He enhanced the brother's work to the detriment of his own."

This is what love looked like for the desert Christians. The particular magic of the desert was its opening an alternative way of being. Not the cutthroat consumerism and competition of the marketplace—to which even these two men were directing their energies—but the sacrificial giving and prioritizing of another's needs over one's own.

Another story tells of a brief conversation during which people may have been discussing love. It charms me to think that these desert dwellers, many of them men, may have done this occasionally: gathered to talk about love! In this conversation, one of the men simply asked, "Do you know what love is?" and then proceeded to define love with a story in which a man named Agathon was admired for the "fine little knife" he owned and pressed the person who admired it into taking it.

That all three of these stories involve material things is important. Each story conveys through brief interaction around material objects—a brick, baskets and their handles, a knife—how love might be expressed and felt. Perhaps the most telling unifying factor in these stories is that they all present these interactions around material objects as failing to be contentious, as failing to demonstrate the ownership so common in their cultural context and in our own.

THE PARADOXICAL PLAY OF DECEPTION AS LOVE?

I'VE LONG BEEN FASCINATED BY THE STORIES of deception—like that involved with the basket handles above—that are sprinkled throughout these story collections. They appear countercultural even within the Christian desert tradition, because the desert Christians seem otherwise to have valued radical self-honesty with themselves, God, and others. This radical openness led directly to the sacrament of confession and practices of spiritual direction still common in some Christian traditions today.[6] The stories of deception, however, show that love can require modes of self-disclosure or self-inhibition at times, given the exigencies of the moment and another person's need.

For instance, when a group of desert Christians were once traveling, they apparently were being led by someone who didn't know the way very well. Instead of shaming the leader and questioning his fitness for leadership, the group seems to have conferred and come up with the idea that one of them would feign being sick so that they would all have to stop for the night and wait until it became light enough to see better. They did this, staying there until dawn, the story goes, "and did not put the brother to shame."[7]

Another story tells of how an exhausted desert Christian named Paphnoutios happened upon a band of robbers drinking wine. Apparently, one of the robbers knew Paphnoutios didn't drink wine and so used his weapon to force Paphnoutios to slake his thirst. This story likely presents Paphnoutios as the exemplar of love for being willing to break his ascetic commitment to obey another, but we also see how the robber himself exercised love in forcing Paphnoutios against his will to do what was best for him in his exhaustion. That he only *feigned* threat of violence adds somehow to the playful magic of this story and how it worked between the men to preserve a sense of one man's integrity as an ascetic and another man's integrity as a threatening, violence-prone, though paradoxically loving, outlaw.

For me, these stories shimmer with the heat of desert light and sun. They offer surprising visions that change with a slant of perspective from one angle to another. The mirage of desert heat and light often offered the desert Christians tempting visions of a life they left behind for the good of their souls. There is so much everyday deception in our world, from imposter syndrome to fake news, from the advice of "fake it 'til you make it" to photoshopped images and videos. The emergence of ChatGPT and other artificial-intelligence tools will continue to make our discernment of the real and the false more difficult. It seems useful for me to consider stories in which deception was playfully and lovingly engaged for the sake of another. They show us the very real unreality of ownership, the insubstantiality of our performing roles of consumer/producer in the worlds we've created and inhabit now, and our deep reliance on one another and on the land that loves us like a mother.

Contemplation Is the Marrow

By Adam Bucko

ONTEMPLATION IS NOT A FRINGE PART of Christianity. It is
Christianity—lived deeply. Christian meditation and contemplative
practice are not side dishes or optional enhancements. They are
the marrow, not the margins, of Christian life. This isn't something new. This
tradition—this living stream—begins with Jesus, flows through the desert
fathers and mothers, continues through monastic life, and is still alive today.

From the beginning, the Christian life was shaped by the rhythm Jesus
himself modeled—a life of action flowing from deep stillness. He withdrew
to pray alone. He took his friends up the mountain to witness transfigura-
tion. He sought the silence of the wilderness. Clearly, something transformative happened when Jesus stepped away, and those around him recognized that his outward life was rooted in his inward union with God.

In the early centuries of Christianity, this pattern took on clearer shape in the deserts of Egypt, Palestine, and Syria. The desert mothers and fathers retreated from the cities to resist the empire's distortions of the Gospel. After Constantine's conversion and the Church's increasing entanglement with imperial power, many felt that something essential was being lost. So, they left—not to flee reality, but to seek it more deeply. Into caves, huts, and small communities, they went to remember, to pray, to live simply, and to wrestle with God.

Their withdrawal was an act of protest and purification. They sought not an abstract inner peace, but the kind of stillness that allows for communion—with God, with self, and eventually, with others. What they forged was not a rejection of the world but a different way of living in it.

What began with Jesus and took clearer shape in the desert then moved West—and began to flourish in new forms. Viewed from a Western monastic perspective, the stream of contemplation flowed through the deserts of the East and eventually exploded into a variety of expressions in Europe. Of course, there are many contemplative traditions—one might say as many as there are people and communities seeking to live in awareness of God's presence. While we are held by a shared tradition and a common rhythm of prayer, the way this life unfolds can take many forms. The goal has never been to crack some contemplative code or become fluent in the mechanics of prayer. It has always been to become the kind of person who lives awake to God's presence—in a way that is rooted, communal, and yet responsive to the unique textures of our lives, cultures, and communities.

The community I belong to—the Community of the Incarnation—seeks to follow this ancient path and renew it for our time. We are a new monastic community rooted in the Christian contemplative tradition, drawing from the insights of the early desert dwellers while translating them into forms that can be lived in everyday life. Inspired by what Fr. Bede Griffiths (1906–1993) called "the universal call to contemplation,"[1] we affirm that intimacy

The Franciscan tradition brought the insights of contemplative experience into direct relationship with creation and poverty.

with God is not the domain of a spiritual elite but is available to all. Our practice democratizes the gifts of monastic spirituality and engages them with the longings and challenges of the world we live in today. We are a dispersed community with members across North America.

This living tradition first reached the West through figures like John Cassian (c.360–c.435), who traveled from Gaul to the Egyptian desert in the late fourth century. Cassian lived among the desert elders, listened carefully, and brought their teachings back to the Latin-speaking world. His *Conferences* and *Institutes* became foundational texts that shaped the Rule of St. Benedict and the entire landscape of Western monasticism.

Benedict, writing in the sixth century, didn't offer grand mystical systems or theories about prayer. He wrote a simple, practical guide for living a life centered on God, in community. He had lived as a hermit, but he realized that many people who went off alone—without guidance—were getting spiritually lost. What he offered instead was a balanced way of life rooted in communal stability, humility, and attentiveness.

The Rule of St. Benedict is earthy and grounded. It talks about how to eat and sleep, how to pray and work, how to listen and speak, how to be present, and how to be silent. It's a recipe for becoming present—to God, to one another, and to life itself. Benedictine spirituality does not abandon the world. It seeks to transfigure the world through attention, simplicity, and presence. Benedict took the radical impulse of the desert and brought it into a life that could be lived in relationship—with others, with time, and with the sacred.

In the sixteenth century, the Carmelite tradition, as reformed by Teresa of Ávila and John of the Cross, offered another essential layer to the contemplative path. Their teachings, rooted in the ancient Carmelite lineage going back to Mount Carmel in the Holy Land, helped articulate the inner map of the soul. They offered language for what happens in the interior life—dryness, ecstasy, detachment, darkness, union—and taught how to navigate the landscape of the heart.

The Franciscan tradition brought the insights of contemplative experience into direct relationship with creation and poverty. St. Francis of Assisi (c. 1181–1226) lived as if the whole world was his monastery. His spirituality was rooted in joy, simplicity, and kinship—with lepers, birds, the poor, and the earth itself. He showed us that contemplation was not only meant to be turned inward but lived outwardly in radical love.

This particular configuration—drawing from Benedictine, Carmelite, and Franciscan spirituality—shapes our life together in the Community of the Incarnation. These three streams form a path of prayer and action, contemplation, and compassion.

Our life is also shaped by three accountabilities. First, we hold ourselves accountable to God and to each other through the spiritual disciplines of the Twelve Steps—a path of honesty, vulnerability, and ongoing conversion of life. Second, we are accountable to the earth, embracing an earth-centered spirituality that sees the natural world as a sacred text, a place of divine presence, not just raw material. And third, we are accountable to the poor, guided by liberation theology and liberation spirituality—hearing and responding to the cry of the poor and the cry of the earth—not as separate, but as one cry.

This, for us, is contemplation lived. It's not about disappearing into mystical experiences. It's about being formed into people who can show up—fully, truthfully, lovingly—in a suffering world.

We're not alone in drawing from such contemporary tools. The contemplative tradition is a living tradition. Each generation is called to renew it—not by making it up from scratch, but by entering a deep and honest conversation with it, allowing it to speak into the longings and wounds of the present moment, and letting those contemporary questions reshape how the tradition lives. In that spirit, we find ourselves responding to the urgent needs of our time—reforming some of the life-denying tendencies of Western spirituality that disconnect soul from body, contemplation from action, and religion from justice. In an age of ecological crisis, systemic injustice, and deep loneliness, we need a spirituality that engages the world, not escapes it.

That's why we benefit from the gifts of modern psychology, trauma healing, somatic awareness, neuroscience, and present-day social analysis. These tools were not available to the early monastics—but they don't replace the tradition. They help us embody it more fully. The containers we've inherited—monastic rules, rhythms of prayer, sacred texts—are powerful, but they were shaped in times when we knew less about how trauma lives in the body or how systems of oppression affect the soul. So, we add to them. We draw on psychotherapy and body-based practices and on the Twelve Steps, which offer a structure for welcoming powerlessness, confession, mutual support, and surrender. These newer insights help us stay grounded, honest, and free.

Oneing
18

One of the elders who has helped me live into this integrative approach—studying the tradition deeply while also reimagining it for today—has been Matthew Fox. His Four Paths framework was especially helpful to me in naming the shape of a spiritual life that is both rooted in tradition and responsive to the world we live in.

It began to take shape after a turning point in Fox's life: During a serious surgery, he had a powerful experience of the presence of Dominican Meister Eckhart (1260–1328). Though Fox himself is a Dominican, he realized—almost with disbelief—that the work of this towering mystic had never been part of his formal theological education.

That moment touched something deep. While still recovering in the hospital, Fox began diving into Eckhart's writings in Latin and German. From that immersion and from Fox's own experience as a spiritual theologian and teacher, he began to articulate a framework for the spiritual life that felt more grounded in the fullness of the Christian tradition—and more urgently needed for our time.

He called it the Four Paths: the via positiva, the way of delight and awe; the via negativa, the way of silence, darkness, letting go, and grief; the via creativa, the path of cocreation, imagination, and generativity; and the via transformativa, the call to respond to injustice with compassion and prophetic action.

In many ways, this is a needed corrective to the dominant medieval framework of the spiritual journey: purgation, illumination, and union. That classic threefold path—shaped by Pseudo-Dionysius and later developed by mystics and scholastics—has been meaningful for many, but it often centers the journey on sin, brokenness, and purification. It begins with the problem. Fox's framework begins with innate goodness—with the sacredness of creation. It reminds us that before there was sin, there was that original goodness. In Genesis 1, God calls creation "good" and humanity "very good." That has to matter.

In a time like ours, this recentering feels not just helpful but necessary. The question before us is not only about our woundedness or sin—it's also about our inherent dignity, about the divine image that is never erased, about what is still beautiful, still possible, still holy—within us and around us. It's this emphasis on sacredness and possibility that has drawn others to Fox's vision.

Contemplation is not about escaping life but entering it more fully.

German liberation theologian and mystic Dorothee Sölle (1929–2003) saw Fox's framework as essential for our time. She believed it gave us a way of doing spirituality that stays connected to justice and to the suffering of the world—a spirituality that can engage in the work of social and ecological transformation, not just personal enlightenment. And she recognized, as did Fox, that this isn't something new—it's what we see in Jesus. His life wasn't only about personal purification. It was about joy, relationship, resistance, and healing. His was a life of deep presence and courageous love.

Fox's framework makes room for woundedness and sin, but it doesn't center it. It makes room for lament and loss but reminds us to begin with awe. It opens us to a spirituality that is not just about escape or transcendence, but about incarnation, about showing up to this world, in its beauty and its brokenness, as lovers, creators, and coconspirators with God.

Contemplation, then, is not a separate path or a unique calling. It is Christianity itself, lived with depth and honesty. It is the heart of the Christian tradition, stretching from Jesus to the desert to today. And as our understanding of the human person has deepened—through psychology, neuroscience, and trauma studies—we are invited to add new tools, not because the tradition was wrong, but because it was formed in a different time, with less knowledge of how we carry and transmit pain. These new tools help us to heal, to stay present, and to love more freely.

In the end, contemplation is not about escaping life but entering it more fully. It is how we listen for God in the silence—and how we hear God in the cries of the poor, the groaning of creation, and the joy of being alive. It is how we remember what's good and live from that place for the sake of the world.

Tradition in One Hand, Evolution in the Other:

The Ongoing Renewal of Christian Monastic Spirituality

By Katie Gordon

"**K**ATIE, KATIE, KATIE—I need to tell you about the Goddess of *Transformation*!"

Standing in the doorway of our shared office, above the light-switch, is a wooden sculpture of Kali, the Hindu Goddess of Transformation. My new officemate, Sr. Carolyn, pointed to her and said, "Every time you come in and flip on the switch, or go out and flip it off, I want you to remember, Katie! *God is change.* We are all evolving, growing. We are never done changing!"

If we only ever preach one sermon in life, this was Sr. Carolyn's: God is change, and we are always changing. She found inspiration for this not just in her own tradition of Benedictine Christian spirituality, but also through other great spiritual traditions.

I had just moved into the Pax Priory, an intentional living community that the Benedictine Sisters of Erie started in 1972 as a peace and non-violence center in the city. Carolyn, a Benedictine Sister in her eighties, had been one of the original residents there. Meanwhile, I was more spiritual-but-not-religious, though raised Catholic, in my early thirties, and the house's newest resident.

When I moved in, she invited me to share this office with her. She was wrapping up a lifetime of teaching and leading creation-spirituality retreats, and I was organizing with younger generations to create new containers for spiritual community in response to the longings of today.

Looking back on our convent corner office, I can see all the ways we stood on the threshold of a living tradition—between the past and the future, between our generations, and between our expressions of the monastic call.

The former monastery where Pax is located was originally built in 1890 and housed the nuns until they established a new monastery outside the city seventy-five years later. Several sisters, though, proposed that there must be community that remained in the heart of the inner city: a center for justice where lay and religious, men and women, guests and seekers all lived together.

That is how it came to be that in the halls where, once upon a time, nuns in habits observed the Grand Silence, there is now laughter ringing through the rafters from the kids in the daycare program on the first two floors. On the grand wooden staircase once meticulously cleaned with toothbrushes by the sisters, the kids now run up and down, speaking the several languages of the migrant communities represented in the program.

Just upstairs, there are offices for several ministries that evolved out of the sisters' faithful presence in the city, including a soup kitchen and food pantry, an online monastery of contemporary seekers, and an association of monasteries sharing resources across the globe. These might hardly be recognizable to the original sisters who settled here in the 1850s to educate German immigrants, but they are nonetheless extensions of the same call to community and ministry, yet in a new era of need.

This former monastery building and all the new life within it is just one fractal of the transformation of religion and spirituality today. With tradition in one hand and evolution in the other, Christian monasticism's spirit of *conversatio*, or continual change, continues to pull us into the future.

———

T HERE ARE THREE VOWS that Benedictines take when they profess their commitment. Rather than the celibacy, poverty, and obedience of most apostolic or "active" orders, the monastic vows are stability, *conversatio*, and obedience.

Stability is the monk's commitment to community, to deepening in a particular place and with a particular group of people. It means that even amid restlessness, I will choose to stay rooted here.

Conversatio is Latin for conversion of life, and it asks the monk to remain open to the continual change or conversions of life. This promise today is called "fidelity to the monastic way of life" and is practiced as a faithfulness amidst the reality of constant change.

Finally, obedience is a practice for continual listening: within, to community, and to the signs of the times. Benedictines in particular are inspired by the first words of the Rule of Benedict: "*Listen with the ear of your heart.*" This listening is not for following orders, but for following the spirit.

These three vows together make for a dynamic life: continually evolving, yet with a steady heart. Out of one's grounded and centered life, change becomes easier to navigate, and the cries of one's own heart and the cries of the world become easier to hear.

In short, the monk is someone who teaches us about ongoing renewal.

Even the early monastics reveal this to us. In the midst of Christianity's growing political influence in the fourth century, after Constantine laid the groundwork to make Christianity the state religion and therefore a tool of power and war, some walked away from urban state religion. These walkouts viewed Christianity's marriage with state power as a corruption of a faith that was meant to follow Jesus's example and question the politics of the era. Those people who walked away from the corruption of faith in the city were the early monks.

In the desert, they established alternative societies more aligned with the life of Jesus. Over the centuries, they practiced what it meant to live the Christian faith together. They wrote and rewrote rules of life to sustain them in human community. The Rule that has lasted since the sixth century, and that is read today in the community I live in, came from this great era of monastic experimentation.

Rooted in this countercultural history, monastic spirituality is on the renewing edge of the Christian tradition. Like the early monks who left the city to practice their faith more authentically in the desert, monasteries to this day are located outside of the hierarchical power of the church. Rather than locate their authority from the institution itself, they gain their authority from their daily living of the faith and their following of a rule of life.

The monastic is someone who is on the edge of the tradition. Richard Rohr might call this the "edge of the inside": not located safely within the hierarchical institution, nor a contrarian throwing rocks at it from the outside. The monastic is neither inside nor outside, but on the threshold between. The monastic holds onto tradition in one hand and evolution in the other.

From the beginning, monastics have been on the renewing edge of the Christian tradition. Like anyone, though, monks need to remember what that asks of us. We need to recall the practices of renewal already within our tradition.

———

T O REMAIN ON THIS RENEWING EDGE takes commitment. It takes practice to not grow complacent. To keep embracing change requires exercising that muscle. Renewal is not a one-time event, something implemented and completed. Renewal is an ongoing practice. It is the reality of being a living tradition.

A core practice of renewal in the monastery is the daily reading of the Rule of Benedict, along with insight from a contemporary commentary: Tradition in one hand, evolution in the other.

Benedict knows that to be in a monastery is to be experimenting, evolving, and even expanding.

Every morning, as we begin community prayer, we read from the Rule of Life written over 1,500 years ago by Benedict of Nursia (480–547), that early monk who sought to formalize the communal monastic life into a model for others. This Rule wasn't simply based in theory or theology, but in practice and lived experience. While we do not know for sure, we can imagine it being written after a life of experimentation, which no doubt included mishaps and failures. The Rule became a blueprint for creating and sustaining spiritual community.

In the monastery, this is the rule we read from every day. Taken a few paragraphs at a time, it takes about four months to read through the seventy-three brief chapters, meaning the Rule is read in its entirety three times a year.

After the Rule is read aloud, a contemporary commentary is read. From the perspectives of monastics living in our own era, we hear about an ongoing wrestling with the text and teachings. We hear interpretations of the Rule that help us bridge these ancient standards into our own contexts. We hear diverse voices pushing up against and translating its wisdom into the complexity of our own century.

This Rule is not meant to be set in stone, expecting rigid adherence, rooted in a previous era. Rather, the Rule is better understood as providing guidelines or guardrails for whole and holy living. Benedict embraces flexibility in the Rule, like in Chapter 40 on "The Quantity of Drink." Rather than determine the exact measure of food and drink, he lays down general advice, followed by the caveat that a superior can shift expectations based on local conditions. Benedict sets up enough structure to allow for adaptability with its implementation.

The Rule itself, the commentaries, and our own regular rereading create a renewing practice for the ways in which a monastic expresses the tradition. When we return to the text again and again, we are bound to uncover new insights each time.

And in the final chapter, Benedict tells the reader: This is just the beginning. Go and read more monastic texts from other sources, he suggests. Go back and read this again, he encourages. Benedict knows that to be in a monastery is to be experimenting, evolving, and even expanding.

T HE CHRISTIAN MONASTIC tradition began with an experiment in a new way of living. In the desert, more experiments ensued— there were hermits in caves, villages of monks and seekers, and cenobites living in community at a monastery. Over the centuries, monasticism formalized a structure, transforming into a tradition that could be passed down from age to age, that could help it to spread from place to place.

Monastics today have inherited both a living tradition and an institution. Ideally, one feeds the other. Possibly, one destroys the other. The institution can smother the living tradition, or the living tradition can die out if there is no way to practice it or pass it on.

This is why the monastic holds onto both tradition and evolution. The monk needs the vows for stability *and* for conversion. The monk needs the Rule *and* the commentary. Ultimately, the monk needs the monastery *and* the world.

Back on that first day at Pax, Carolyn led me out of the office doors to complete the tour. "Do you see this framed picture?" she asked, pausing in the doorway and pointing above her. I looked up and saw an image of the earth as seen from space. "This picture is our home, *the wider world*. It is a reminder for you every time you walk in or out of these doors," Carolyn told me.

"I want you to always remember you are a *part* of this world. We, as monastics, are *changed by* the world. We are *changing* the world. When we are here in the monastery, we are not apart from the world but wrapped up in it! When we walk into the world, we must remember: We are not alone. We are all connected."

The Living Tradition of Black Contemplative Preaching

By E. Trey Clark

INTRODUCTION

I N HER GROUNDBREAKING BOOK, *Joy Unspeakable*, the Rev. Dr. Barbara Holmes (1943–2024) reminds us of the expansiveness of contemplation, especially within Black cultural contexts.[1] For her, contemplation calls us not to otherworldly escape, but this-worldly engagement. In other words, it is a practice of sacred seeing that emerges from and contributes to engagement with God in the concrete realities of our times. Amid the many social, political, and ecological challenges in our world, it is essential to learn from traditions of contemplation that offer wisdom for how to hold together prayer and public witness. Alongside other minoritized contemplative traditions, the Black church[2] has much to offer in this regard. In this essay, I examine one of the lesser-known contemplative practices in the Black church—contemplative preaching.[3]

In Christian faith traditions, contemplative preaching is a mode of proclamation that weds prayer, wisdom, and reflection to invite listeners into a transformative encounter with God for the good of the world and the glory of God. It manifests in various ways in different cultural and social contexts. For our purposes, I am particularly interested in contemplative preaching as it is often practiced by people of African descent in the United States— what I call Black contemplative preaching.[4] While similar to contemplative preaching more broadly, Black contemplative preaching is shaped by the holistic spirituality, communal orientation, and vibrant orality that is part of the rich Africana heritage—even when embodied outside of predominantly Black contexts. Moreover, Black contemplative preaching unites the head and the heart, the personal and the communal, and spiritual formation and social transformation as it bears witness to the liberating and life-giving gospel of Jesus Christ. While recognizing that contemplation is ultimately a gift, Black contemplative preachers seek to guide people to experience loving communion with the divine, while also pursuing the flourishing of Black people and all of God's creation. In the remainder of this essay, I explore Black contemplative preaching as a living tradition that can inspire prophetic witness in the face of the challenges of our contemporary moment.

To begin, it is essential to note that Black contemplative preaching is not a recent development. Its deep roots can be traced to the lineage of biblical prophets such as Moses, Isaiah, Mary, and Jesus himself. Moreover, it stems from a tradition of African mystics, including St. Anthony, Moses the Black, and St. Mary of Egypt. It is also part of a larger history of mystic preachers in the Christian tradition that includes Augustine of Hippo, Hildegard of Bingen, St. Francis of Assisi, Meister Eckhart, Dona Beatriz Kimpa Vita, and others. While I have explored some of this history elsewhere,[5] here I would like to highlight two historical exemplars of Black contemplative preaching from the modern era: Sojourner Truth and Howard Thurman.

S OJOURNER TRUTH (c. 1797–1883) was born into slavery as Isabella Bomefree (also spelled Baumfree or Baumfrey).[6] Early on, her faith was nurtured in the Dutch Reformed Church and a mystic community known as the Zion Hill communal group. However, she eventually joined the African Methodist Episcopal Zion (AMEZ) denomination. Throughout her life, she faced profound suffering—including enslavement, rape, and libel. For her, a life of prayer became a means of survival and empowerment. In fact, somewhat like St. Mary of Egypt and other desert mothers, she chose a secluded place in nature for prayer to which "she resorted daily, and in pressing times more frequently."[7] Reflecting on Isabella's practice of prayer in nature, Joy Bostic wrote that she cultivated the habit of contemplating the "expansiveness of the One who created the heavens and the earth."[8]

Isabella's life of contemplation provided the spiritual strength, wisdom, and insight to engage in courageous proclamation. Later, on the day of Pentecost, June 1, 1843, she changed her name to Sojourner Truth to reflect her sense of call to preach God's truth amid deception and injustice. While unable to read or write, Truth was a profound spiritual preacher who some-times would say to people she knew: "You read books; God himself talks to me."[9] Her most well-known speech, often described as "Ain't I a Woman," emerged from her practice of embodied contemplation and observation of life and the story of Scripture. Some scholars have argued that Truth likely did not use the phrase "ain't I a woman" (or "ar'nt I a woman").[10] Still, in this iconic message, we find a reliable glimpse into how she lamented the mistreatment she and other Black women faced at the time and called her listeners into a different way of seeing and being. In the speech, she proclaimed:

> Nobody ever helps me into carriages, or over mud-puddles, or gives me any best place! And ain't I a woman? Look at me! Look at my arm! I have ploughed and planted, and gathered into barns, and no man could head me! And ain't I a woman?... Then that little man in black there, he says women can't have as much rights as men, 'cause Christ wasn't a woman! Where did your Christ come from? Where did your Christ come from? From God and a woman! Man had nothing to do with Him.[11]

Sojourner Truth speaks these words as one who had gazed upon God and knew that she was beloved. As a result, she calls her audience to cultivate a "nonviolent gaze" of contemplation that subverts the sexist and racist ways Black women were viewed and treated.[12] And she does this through making a theological argument—Christ came into the world through "God and a woman."[13] The boldness of Truth's proclamation reflects her union of contemplation and action, which fueled her pursuit of justice and equity for Black women.

HOWARD THURMAN AS CONTEMPLATIVE PREACHER

THE SECOND HISTORICAL EXEMPLAR of contemplative preaching that I would like to note is Howard Washington Thurman (1899–1981).[14] Born in Daytona Beach, Florida, Thurman lived a long life as an African American mystic, theologian, pastor, and spiritual mentor or guide to countless activists in the civil rights movement—including Pauli Murray, Jesse Jackson, and Congressman John Lewis. Throughout his formative years, Thurman experienced intense racism and segregation that "left its scars deep in [his] spirit."[15] However, on his journey, rather than dehumanizing those who oppressed Black folks and others, he never relented in pursuing what he described as "the search for common ground."[16] As part of his search, Thurman cofounded one of the first intentionally intercultural, interracial, interfaith congregations in the US: the Church for the Fellowship of All Peoples. Reflecting on his preaching ministry, Thurman once stated: "The core of my preaching has always concerned itself with the development of the inner resources needed for the creation of a friendly world of friendly [people]."[17] In other words, he sought to help people cultivate a robust interior life with God that would enrich their engagement with others around them.

However, Thurman's sermons did not merely challenge people to seek the flourishing of other humans. He also invited people to live out what Douglas Christie has called "a contemplative ecological vision," that is, a vision that calls for a different way of seeing and being that supports creation's flourishing.[18] For instance, a few months after the celebration of the first Earth Day in April 1970, Thurman preached a sermon at Colonial Church of Edina, Minnesota (now known as Meetinghouse Church), entitled "Jesus and the Natural Order." In the sermon, he proclaimed: "In our power over

Sojourner Truth calls her audience to cultivate a "nonviolent gaze" of contemplation that subverts the sexist and racist ways Black women were viewed and treated.

nature, and in our radical unremembering of the fact that we are a part of nature, we feel that we can abuse nature.... But in truth we are of the essence of the ebb and flow of the heartbeat of nature, so that we cannot do violence to nature without there being an echo of agony moving through all the corridors of the spirit."[19] Thurman's words reveal his conviction that humans and the more-than-human creation are in an interdependent relationship. For him, this fact has ethical consequences for how we live. His sermon reflects his commitment to inviting listeners to the kind of spiritual life that contributed to the flourishing of all God's creation. Although Thurman died in 1981, his voice remains as relevant as ever to the hungry hearts of a new generation of contemplative activists engaged in various forms of proclamation, within and outside of congregational contexts.

CONTEMPORARY CONTEMPLATIVE PREACHERS

ONE NOTABLE CONTEMPORARY EXEMPLAR of Black contemplative preaching is Pastor Tia Norman. Norman serves as the lead pastor of Awakenings in Houston, Texas, a community whose vision is to "serve as a global community using contemplative spirituality to heal, renew, and inspire."[20] The sermons at Awakenings are often described as "Truth Communications." Rather than a monologue, the messages tend to create sacred space for reflection, dialogue, and communal spiritual practices.

Amid the intense fear and instability for many in the aftermath of the 2025 presidential inauguration, Awakenings offered a teaching series on Grounds for Liberation. In one message entitled "When Oppression Pushes Back," Norman explored the story of the intensification of the Israelites' oppression under Pharoah in Egypt as recorded in Exodus 5.[21] She suggested that similar to the Israelites' experience, many folks in our society today experience what Howard Thurman called "a war of nerves" that leads them to lean on fear as an understandable yet unreliable "safety device."[22] As a counter to fear, Norman invited the community to identify and share a Scripture passage, song, poem, or something in nature that reminded them of their "authentic signature" as a beloved child of God.[23] In a context of profound systemic injustice, she offered a timely contemplative sermon that helped people to find grounding in their inner life to engage their outer life more faithfully.

Of course, there are many other Black exemplars of contemplative preaching in the present. For example, I think of the contemplative proclamation of the Rev. adwoa Wilson at St. Michael's Episcopal Church in Brattleboro, Vermont; the Rev. Dr. Luke Powery at Duke Chapel in Durham, North Carolina; and the Rev. Dr. Jay Williams at Union Church in Boston, Massachusetts. Outside of ecclesial contexts, I am struck by how the Los Angeles-based poet and activist Amanda Gorman offers contemplative sermonizing through her deeply moving poetry.[24] While these individuals may not describe themselves as contemplative preachers, it is noteworthy how each of them, in their own way, offers proclamation that emerges from and encourages sacred seeing that contributes to the good of the world.

BLACK CONTEMPLATIVE INSPIRATION FOR TODAY

L ET ME CONCLUDE by reflecting on a few ways the living tradition of Black contemplative preaching can inspire prophetic witness today. First, contemplative preachers challenge us to move beyond "dualistic thinking" and embrace paradox and ambiguity instead.[25] For the contemplative preacher, God meets us in the mystery and messiness of life. Thus, as Frank Thomas notes, contemplative sermons courageously name "both hope and despair, the absence and the presence of God" that are inescapable realities of human existence.[26] In an age of longing for depth rather than simplistic answers, we need such sermons, preached in word and deed, more than ever.

Second, related to this, in a world full of painful divisions and hate, contemplative preachers invite us to embody boundary-breaking community. Without ignoring acute differences that have consequential social implications, Black contemplatives tend to be oriented toward recognizing and affirming oneness. As a result, they preach, teach, and lead in a way that calls us again and again to the work of building the kind of loving community "where always the boundaries are giving way to the coming of others from beyond them—unknown and undiscovered [siblings]."[27]

Finally, amid a culture of overwork, contemplative preachers challenge us to not let the pace at which we do the work of God destroy God's work in us.[28] There are endless urgent and important issues, causes, and needs in our time. And yet, Black contemplatives remind us even Jesus had moments when he would "withdraw to deserted places and pray" (Luke 5:16, NRSV). Truly, in our capitalistic society, as Tricia Hersey puts it, "rest is resistance."[29] If we are to embody and engage the living tradition of Black contemplative preaching, we would do well to remember that faithful ministry requires discerning healthy rituals of replenishment that can sustain us on our journey.

Queering the
Living Tradition

By Cassidy Hall

I WAS IN MY EARLY THIRTIES and at a crossroads in life. I was flailing, stuck in a holding pattern I couldn't break through. Working as a counselor, I was burnt out, overworked, constantly behind, and starting to have panic attacks. I couldn't break through to the other side—I had no idea what the other side even was.

I began to notice I not only felt stuck, I also felt distant from my true self. I was in a world where I didn't belong, because I had yet to fully belong to myself. I had accepted myself as a queer woman, but I wasn't allowing my whole self to exist in the world in all of the ways that made me, *me*.

Between clients, I wrestled with what to do. One day, I looked to my desk and saw *New Seeds of Contemplation*, a book by the Trappist monk Thomas Merton (1915–1968). To this day, I have no idea where the book came from.

I can't recall if I found it or if someone gave it to me. As I read it, every page resonated with something deep in my soul that had yet to be touched, yet to be met, yet to be explored. *Something* finally made sense. Though I was queer and not Catholic, the words of this Trappist monk piqued my curiosity. Thinking about the fullness of my true self not only as a queer woman but also as someone feeling stuck in life, I read these words from an essay aptly titled *Integrity*:

> Many poets are not poets for the same reason that many religious [people] are not saints: they never succeed in being themselves. They never get around to being the particular poet or the particular monk they are intended to be by God. They never become the [person] or the artist who is called for by all the circumstances of their individual lives. They waste their years in vain effort to be some other poet, some other saint.[1]

It was as if my soul jolted awake. I realized I was trying to be someone else, someone I didn't even know. I discovered Merton had lived in a monastery in Kentucky, 650 miles from my desk in Iowa. In a desperate attempt to chase the resonance of his words for my own life, I quit my job and started to travel across the country to these places I knew next to nothing about—monasteries, specifically Trappist monasteries.

Walking into these spaces, some as old as the late seventeenth century, felt like being in a museum. The monks are known for their daily rhythm of working, reading, and pausing to pray seven times a day. Holding a reverence, I basked in the day's simplicity: *ora et labora*, work and prayer. I regularly joined the prayers until I learned the rhythm I needed: walking, praying, writing, reading. In every monastery, the resonance persisted: I found the silence to be challenging and refreshing, beautiful and painful. The love of the whole world existed right next to all its suffering. The silence of my mind one minute would burst into chaos the next. I sensed the silence held everything and nothing. In solitude, I experienced an inexplicable reality in the unknown, and the paradoxes captivated me.

But the stuckness kept showing up. In the middle of the journey, while at New Clairvaux Abbey in Vina, California, I went on a walk, tortured by the idea that my life was continually aimless. *Why did I quit my job for this? Why am I just reading, writing, and bathing in silence? What a horrifically privileged thing to do! What does this all mean?* I couldn't help but think my stuckness had only guided me into more stuckness, and I'd only abandoned responsibilities. To anyone on the outside looking in on my life, I probably seemed to be encountering a premature midlife crisis. Who would quit a reliable job with health insurance? Who would spend their savings on this bizarre six-month journey?

During this walk, I began asking God these questions. Next thing I knew, I had fallen to my knees on the gravel, weeping with some sense of knowing. I suddenly knew I was going the right way, but I had no idea where I was going. I was no longer just captivated by the paradoxes. I was beginning to live into them.

Reaching into my pocket, I pulled out and unfolded a small piece of paper where I had written a prayer I kept returning to by Thomas Merton:

> My Lord God,
> I have no idea where I am going.
> I do not see the road ahead of me.
> I cannot know for certain where it will end.
> Nor do I really know myself,
> and the fact that I think I am following your will
> does not mean that I am actually doing so.
> But I believe that the desire to please you
> does in fact please you.
> And I hope I have that desire in all that I am doing.
> I hope that I will never do anything apart from that desire.
> And I know that if I do this you will lead me by the right road,
> though I may know nothing about it.
> Therefore will I trust you always though
> I may seem to be lost and in the shadow of death.
> I will not fear, for you are ever with me,
> and you will never leave me to face my perils alone.[2]

Merton wrote these words between 1953 and 1954 in his first hermitage space—an abandoned toolshed on the monastery property he came to name St. Anne's. At the age of thirty-seven, Merton felt something similar to my own experience, writing from the toolshed that it was the first time in his life that he had "a real conviction of doing what I am really called by God to do. It is the first time I have 'arrived'—like a river that has been running through a deep canyon and now has come out in the plains—and is within sight of the ocean (January 20, 1953)."[3]

Insatiable longing was a pattern in Merton's life, one he seemed to grapple with until his death. At this time, he had already lived at the monastery for over ten years, searching, longing, and praying. But if only for a moment, he felt a sense of "arrival" in that rat-infested toolshed:

> With tremendous relief I have discovered that I no longer need to pretend. Because when you have not found what you are looking for, you pretend in your eagerness to have found it. You act as if you had found it. You spend your time telling yourself what you have found and yet do not want. I do not have to buy St. Anne's. I do not have to sell myself to myself here. Everything that was ever real in me has come back to life in this doorway wide open to the sky! I no longer have to trample myself down, cut myself in half, throw part of me out the window, and keep pushing the rest of myself away. In the silence of St. Anne's everything has come together in unity (February 16, 1953).[4]

I had tried too hard to pretend I found what I was looking for in my career and path in life, and the effort had exhausted me. I was finally ready to begin the pursuit of something real, reciprocal, lifegiving—something that doesn't shrink me, destroy my true self, or minimize my personhood.

We may word things differently, but this perpetual search to know the unknowable is a familiar feeling for many contemplatives. We have an almost ravenous hunger, or some might say a palpable thirst, or a seemingly aimless dull ache that thrums through us. The ache reminds us we are in touch with the suffering of the whole world. All contemplatives, no matter their religion or spirituality, seem to have this in common, and recognizing this makes me feel less alone.

The contemplative life is not a way of knowing. It is not the path of certitude. In fact, that's what makes it so alive, so necessarily active. Our glimpses of "arrival" along the way are places we can catch our breath and recall we are moving in the right direction, even if it's only because it's exactly where we are. Those times, we remember that the way is not meant to be easy, simple, or comfortable. But these moments only last for a flash in the midst of life because, as the Rev. Dr. Walter Fluker reminds us, "Life will keep going because life itself is alive."[5]

The contemplative life is not a way of knowing. It is not the path of certitude. In fact, that's what makes it so alive, so necessarily active.

Maybe our moments happen in a place like an abandoned toolshed, or perhaps it's a visceral sense of knowing on a gravel path, but these instances are only signposts along the way, affirming us on the lifelong journey of contemplation—this living, breathing, growing journey. Even though we know the search will never end, the hunt continues. In fact, five years prior to Merton's sense of arrival in St. Anne's, he concluded his best-selling spiritual memoir *The Seven Storey Mountain* by writing in Latin, "*Sit finis libri, non finis quaerendi*," meaning, "Here ends the book, but not the searching."[6]

To *live* within the contemplative tradition is not only to keep searching. It is also an invitation to evolve within and alongside it. We are asked to engage with and deepen into the roots of its origins, while also being called to live into what it looks like in our ever-changing world. The path must grow in order for us to continue on, in order for us to be alive in the living, growing, and breathing tradition. "Living," wrote Merton, "is the constant adjustment of thought to life and life to thought in such a way that we are always growing, always experiencing new things in the old and old things in the new. Thus life is always new."[7]

As captivated as I was by these monasteries and the Christian contemplative tradition, as a queer woman I couldn't see myself within it. My own experience of coming to contemplative Christianity began with predominantly white, usually male, and often celibate teachers. As they lacked any aspect of my own identity, I knew something was missing—*someone* was missing. Many of us were missing. I wasn't hearing from people of color, those on the margins of society, and I wasn't hearing about the queer experience, the ways contemplative life impacts my embodied existence as a person whose sexuality was outside the norm. Once I dug deeper and learned about contemplative Christianity's origins in the deserts of modern-day Palestine, Syria, and Egypt, I started looking for these voices, knowing they had existed since the beginning.

In my research and experience, I've found that we come from all walks of life, cultures, and markers of identity. There is a unity in our uniqueness, and that common thread binds us together, allowing us to recognize each other.

In *Joy Unspeakable: Contemplative Practices of the Black Church*, Dr. Barbara Holmes (1943– 2024) wrote of the vastness of contemplative tradition, not just in people but also in experiences. Dr. Holmes reminded us that contemplation can also be "evocative, still or embodied in dance and shout," even saying that it is "mystical, pragmatic, and efficacious."[8] She widened the Christian contemplative path by reminding us to expand the way we think about the involvement of our ancestors, healers, and spirits: "African contemplations acknowledge spiritual entities and energies as part of the everyday world."[9]

As I learned from more diverse voices, I came to understand Christian contemplation as a living tradition. The word *living* insinuates an ongoing, even growing nature. Life necessitates space, breathing room, and an openness to change. That which is living cannot exist in a place of complete certitude — to do so would be to count it dead: not continuing, not evolving, not ever-becoming. In this way, contemplation is its own spiritual paradox, one of tradition and change, stillness and action.

When I think back to my discovery of Merton at my desk in Iowa, I often think about the pilgrims who would travel to the desert elders of the third and fourth centuries, begging for a word of life—a word *alive*, a word *living*. I'm certain that they too felt that dull ache leading them into the desert. I wonder if the words were received as a brief moment of arrival or a signpost of clarity.

The word *queer*, for me, has been one of those words of life. It has offered me a clearer vision of my true self and thus connected me more deeply to the Divine. Words of life are not only markers for the journey but also encouragements toward our own growth, our own living, our own actions in life. Signposts along the way may come in the form of words, places, people, encounters. However they come, our noticing reminds us of who we are, that we're going the right way, and that we aren't alone.

I've come to embrace the word *queer* as both an identity and a lens for the contemplative life. Like the word *living*, the word *queer* offers an aliveness that cannot be contained, not only because of my identity as a queer, but because it is also a word of expanse, much like *living*, or *wild*, or *free*.

I've found comfort in the Christian contemplative tradition. It has offered me a sense of belonging and even agreement. Tradition offers a rhythm that brings me ease. But I have learned that contemplative life cannot be domesticated. It cannot be seen only through the lens of whiteness, patriarchy, heteronormativity, or any other forces of domination or control. For me, to live a contemplative life means to disentangle myself from these norms and expectations. Each contemplative is a widening incarnation of the Divine, an opportunity to examine the Christian contemplative tradition from new angles.

Throughout my monastic travels, I sent postcards back to the workplace I left behind—the place a book appeared on my desk, the place where I came so close to losing myself that I was forced to go find myself. The postcards tell their own story of lostness and growth, of connection and love. They remind me that no matter how far I go, I am always exactly where and who I am. The person who traveled to the monasteries was the same person whose life felt stuck, the same person who began experiencing panic. In fact, I've felt both these feelings many times since the journey started. But as I began accepting and living into the paradoxes, I found that's where my faith—and life—made the most sense. The Christian contemplative tradition has a queer identity of its own: It doesn't fit into a singular view or experience, it isn't binary, and it resists norms, expectations, domination, and control.

I finally came alive in this living tradition by simply discovering I belonged there. Queer people had always belonged there. And, like Merton, I still have no idea where I am going. But I know I'm not going alone.

Sit finis scripturae, non finis quaerendi, meaning, "Here ends the writing, but not the searching."[10]

Crisis Contemplation

By Barbara Holmes

I'M THE DAUGHTER OF GULLAH ANCESTORS, infused generationally with the healing rhythms of drum talk, auntie shamans, and the mysteries of a multivalent universe. According to scientists, we are all from Africa, a continent where the flow of contemplative life is interwoven with the beckoning of talking drums, the bustling of cities, and the passages and communal witness to the difficulties of living post-colonial life. Since we are all daughters of Africa, no matter our skin color, we can access the healing of the drums. We're being called to consider contemplation in the midst of crisis—as an accessible and vibrant response to life, its blessings and travails, and to a God who unleashes life toward its most diverse potentials and practices, even during dark nights of the soul and the oppression of entire communities.

I first recognized the elements of crisis contemplation when I was writing the first edition of *Joy Unspeakable: Contemplative Practices of the Black Church*. Most folks believed that Black religion did not include contemplative practices. We had rousing sermons, amazing choirs, and evocative worship, but not contemplative practices—not by the standards set by European models.

The image of contemplation most prevalent among us is the lone monastic in prayer, but that's only one type of contemplation. We're used to contemplation as a voluntary and individual turn inward toward sacred reflection and the presence of the source of all being, usually while we're in safe and comfortable spaces. This type of contemplation is exemplified by Teresa of Ávila, St. John of the Cross, Julian of Norwich, and others. Truthfully, contemplation in its historically understood context requires the privilege and time to retreat from the front lines of everyday life, if only for a little while.

For most people and communities under siege, such comforts are inconceivable. Survival requires an alert, spiritual, and embodied stance. When we are in peril, we dare not shift our gaze for even a moment. To contemplate—in the ordinary sense of the word—while in crisis might mean that we misread the signs of our times in our immediate environment. If we're not woke, we might miss the seething resentment just below the surface of a police officer's polite and routine request for driver's license and registration. We might let our guard down at the wrong moment—with lethal consequences.

In the West, our crises tend to be tied to personal needs and troubles. So, I want to be clear that the crisis contemplation I'm writing about is not about the husband or wife who takes you to dinner to ask for a divorce. Sure, that's upsetting, even surprising, but that's not the magnitude that I have in mind. Crisis contemplation is one factor among a series of crises that we can do nothing about.

Crisis doesn't just happen to individuals. It also happens to communities, particularly when a community shatters on the anvil of injustice. Together, a community, when they are in this crisis, engage reflectively and reflexively while transforming and interpreting their circumstances and their relationship with God.

So, what is this crisis contemplation? It is that point of spiritual and psychic dissolution. Shattering events that create the crisis displace the ordinary, until the suffering reaches the point of no return. We are bereft. We are unable to articulate the extent of our suffering or even to reintegrate our fractured meaning structures. The descent begins, and we are in freefall toward the center of our being.

Some historical crises are particularly difficult to hear. When we talk about slavery, the Holocaust, the Trail of Tears, and apartheid, we almost want to shut our ears, as we've heard so much about them. We think to ourselves: "Why do we have to hear about this *again*?" It is not about blame. It is not to assign who's at fault—or not. It is so that we can begin to see with the eyes of the other. We think we know one another, and we really don't.

I used to take students over to Nogales, Sonora, Mexico to experience life in the desert with the poor. They thought they knew what they were going to do: build houses or do missions. When we got there, it took less than three days for the breaking to occur. They did not know what it was like to sleep on a cold dirt floor. They didn't know what it was like to eat a thin soup, called chicken soup, with only a chicken foot in it, for their entire meal. It was an awakening for them.

So, crisis can be personal. This is when the individual has a sense of loss of agency and control, a loss of meaning, a loss of story. We tell ourselves what's real or important and what's not. We tell ourselves who's valuable and who's not. When the crisis is individual, it comes in a number of ways.

There could be a crisis of faith, in God forsaking us, a dark night of the soul, where we have difficulty integrating what is happening to us. I think not just of St. John of the Cross, but also of Mother Teresa, Henri Nouwen, and, in today's context, Bishop Carlton Pearson. Have you seen the film *Come Sunday*? Pearson was a darling of Evangelicals until he gave up on an exclusionary theology and said that God loves all of us. He lost absolutely everything.

Then there's the crisis of testing. It could come in an inexplicable, breaking loss, where you lose everything for seemingly no reason. With this type of loss, I think of Job.

> # Together, a community, when they are in this crisis, engage reflectively and reflexively while transforming and interpreting their circumstances and their relationship with God.

A crisis is not just personal, it's communal. When the crisis is communal, there may be only one cause—injustice, created by systems and societies who impose their will on others with catastrophic results. When the terror becomes unbearable, teachers arise, and representatives of those communities try to lead. They suffer, individually and as members of the afflicted group. I'm thinking of Mahatma Gandhi, Nelson Mandela, Oscar Romero, and Harriet Tubman.

In *Joy Unspeakable*, I use the Black community's experience of slavery as an extreme example of crisis contemplation, a breaking of extraordinary magnitude. When the crisis is communal, communities may be victimized by systems because of immutable traits like race, gender, ethnicity, sexual identity or fluidity, class, political or social differences—real or imagined, and more.

When communities are in crisis, the fear comes first. Perhaps you're Harriet Tubman, hiding and trying to make it to Canada with your community, or you're a person of color today, wondering when the powers that be will decide to put you in the same foil blankets and cages that they're using for Mexican babies.

After the fear comes the cruelty and the oppression, along with the wondering: "Where is God?" Here's the rub: Even as a member of an oppressed community, you're always an individual. But during a crisis of this magnitude, you do not have the luxury of responding as an individual. Suffering in the Holocaust, the Trail of Tears, and slavery, cannot be absorbed by individuals, no matter how tenuous and invisible the bonds of community are. Individuals cannot respond. You must do it as community—for safety, for comfort, and for survival.

So, what happens when a community is in crisis? First, there's rupture from all that is known, all reality structures. There are abrupt transitions, endings and beginnings. Then there is the ritual passage from one reality to another. Finally, there is ineffability, the inability to describe what is happening, and there is forsakenness, writ large.

The first circumstance I'd like to mention is slavery. I'm not going to say a lot about the slavery crisis, simply because we've all heard so much about it that we think we know what's happening. But Africa is not a country like the United States. It's a continent. So, when you take people from Ethiopia, or Ghana, from different countries, you're putting into the hold of a cargo ship people who do not share a language. They do not share religious beliefs.

They do not necessarily share values. It is like putting together Spanish folk and British folk, German folk and Irish folk. What was in the hold of the cargo ships were people who had no ability to communicate with one another. Scholar Anthony Pinn says that the journey, the crisis of soul, spirit, and community, was crucial to the formation of a slave. For had they arrived as strong-minded, strong-bodied Africans, they might have been annihilated upon embarkment. This transition, this chrysalis, this womb in the bottom of a cargo ship, turned them into slaves, so that when they disembarked, they could survive.

The Holocaust is another historical circumstance of crisis contemplation. There are no words to describe the deaths of eleven million people, including six million Jews. So, I reflect on three words: Holocaust, Shoah, and Khurbn. Holocaust comes from the Greek word *holokauston*, which references the great burning, which is difficult to understand, almost as if it was a necessary sacrifice to God—and I cannot imagine what kind of God that would be.

Shoah is the Hebrew word for catastrophe and is the preferred name for the destruction in Israel. A Yiddish word for the Holocaust, Khurbn, comes from the Hebrew word for the destruction of the ancient Temple. This was the word used by survivors of the Holocaust, who often referred to their ordeal as *Letzter Khurbn*, the most recent destruction. This makes sense to me because, as a Christian, I think of the body as a temple. No matter how we describe it, this crisis is beyond comprehension.

A final historical example of crisis that breaks you into contemplation is the Trail of Tears. In 1838 and 1839, Andrew Jackson's Indian Removal Policy was put into place. The Cherokee people called it the Trail of Tears because of its devastating effects. The names of the five tribes were the Cherokee, the Choctaw, the Seminole, the Chickasaw, and the Creek. The Treaty of New Echota in 1835 ceded all Cherokee land to the United States for $5.8 million. That land was then placed in a lottery for white settlers, who drew and received that land.

The Cherokee were not allowed to take extra clothing or food with them. Many died of starvation and malnutrition, and many of the women handed their babies off to African Americans as they were leaving. In my own family, we had a grandfather who was almost six-foot eight. We were all short Gullah people. He had a long, straight braid down his back, and we just called him "Grandpa." We knew he was not of our lineage, but he was received into the arms of one of our Black ancestors and raised as their own.

Now I want to tell you a few of the consequences of being a member of a community in crisis. Dr. Rachel Yehuda, a Professor of Psychiatry, studies epigenetics. She researches how serious incidents of trauma, like slavery and the Holocaust, create post-traumatic stress disorder that can be passed down through generations in families. Her research has revealed that when people experience that kind of trauma, it changes their genes in a very specific and noticeable way. When those people have children, that trauma gene is passed down through the generations.

Yehuda first tested her theory with a very small group of Holocaust survivors, and she found that their hormonal levels and PTSD ratings matched those of Vietnam veterans. As that generation passed away, she met some of the children of the Holocaust survivors, and she thought, "Why don't I check, just to see what their hormonal levels are?" When she did, she found that the traits, the trauma, had been passed down. Although they had not experienced the Holocaust, they had inherited the trauma. It was then that Dr. Joy DeGruy applied the widely accepted research to a phrase she created: post-traumatic slave disorder.

The specific trauma experienced by Black slaves caused immense emotional, physical, and psychological effects, intense enough to cause trauma to survivors. Research is still being done and there is more to be known about how trauma is transmitted. But we do know that when we look at our communities and we ask, "Why are Black people killing Black people in Chicago?" and, "Why is there such a breach of conduct and decency between Israelis and Palestinians?" —sometimes it's inherited trauma.

Fortunately, there is solace during the journey. Crisis contemplation is the breaking, the healing, the transformation of form into substance, façade into meaning, but it is not a space of comfort. It's Ruth and Naomi leaving the comfort of their community. It's Hagar returning to a household where she is not welcome and holding her peace. It's Moses returning to Egypt to demand freedom for his people. It's scary. It's uncomfortable. It's to be avoided at all costs—and yet, it is the only way.

All oppression is connected. It's based on the exercise of unwarranted and ungodly power. It is prolonged, cruel, and unjust treatment. Even during the despair of the community or ethnic groups who are treated unfairly, God is there. During the suffering, we let go and we let God, because even the wrongdoings of others can be used by God for our good. The crisis transforms us. The Holy Spirit empowers us.

I offer here a few examples of how crisis contemplation might be experienced. There is a sense of ineffability that follows the rupture, letting go, freefall, and darkness. Words are useless, will not come to mind, and—even if available—will be of no use. Since the context for the crisis is communal, those in despair want to feel the comfort and presence of those around them, and yet their circumstances will not allow them to communicate in the usual ways. I suggest a few key factors that may arise during crisis contemplation: the eclipse, the moan, and the stillness.

THE ECLIPSE

> There is no chance that we will fall apart
> There is no chance
> There are no parts.
>
> —June Jordan, "Poem Number Two on Bell's Theorem, or The New
> Physicality of Long Distance Love"

IN HER CLEAR, "EVERYDAY" VOICE, poet June Jordan (1936–2002) affirmed the wholeness of everything as a reliable platform of reality. No matter how fractured things seem to be, no matter how the crisis splinters our delusions, there is a solid foundation within and beneath us, beside and between us. We can depend on this wholeness when it is experienced as a dark night of the soul for individuals, or an eclipse of the ordinary for the community.

An eclipse occurs when one object gets in between us and another object and blocks our view. From Earth, we routinely experience two kinds of eclipses: an eclipse of the moon and an eclipse of the sun. Of course, the scientific explanation is more detailed and comprehensive, but for our purposes, what matters most is the sense of temporary absence. We are not permanently blocked from the light. Also, we are not able to rely upon our sight to overcome the obstruction.

Finally, during an eclipse, we have a dimming of the familiar and a loss of taken-for-granted clues that we rely upon every day to remind us of who we are and why we are here. Yet, although we are not always comfortable in darkness, the invitation to come away from life in the spotlight is intriguing. Could there be a blessing in the shadows?

"The eclipse reminds us to linger in the darkness, to savor the silence, to embrace the shadow—for the light is coming, the resurrection is afoot, transformation is unfolding, for God is working in secret and in silence to create us anew."[1]

THE MOAN

I N MY BOOK *Joy Unspeakable*, I rely upon the research of James Noel and my own Middle Passage studies to form a theory about village formation. Noel argued, and I agree, that the moan is the utterance that communicates the ineffability of the crisis, the need to connect to others nearby, and our dependence on a groaning Holy Spirit.

> *We moan to give birth,*
> *to traverse non-linear time,*
> *and to signal movement from*
> *one state of being to another.*
> *We moan as a sign of life,*
> *to give notice to spiritual*
> *bystanders that what looks*
> *like an ending is actually a*
> *beginning.*

In similar fashion, the Holy Spirit groans the prayers for us that we cannot utter while the crisis continues. In the Epistle to the Romans (8:26–27), the apostle Paul states: "In the same way, the Spirit helps us in our weakness. We do not know what we ought to pray for, but the Spirit … intercedes for us through wordless groans."

Throughout chapter 8 in Romans, Paul writes of the sacred utterances of creation and humankind in crisis. We don't know what will emerge from this time of tarrying, but we do know that something is being born. Like a woman in labor, there is expectation in the darkness, anticipation amid the suffering, hope permeating the pain. Something new is being born and something old is being transformed.

In the stillness of quiet, if we listen, we can hear the whisper of the heart giving strength to weakness, courage to fear, hope to despair.

—Howard Thurman

Silence is helpful, but you don't need it to find stillness. Even when there is noise, you can be aware of the stillness underneath the noise, of the space in which the noise arises. That is the inner space of pure awareness, consciousness itself.

—Eckhart Tolle

AFTER THE ECLIPSE and the moan comes the stillness. Stillness and silence are not the same. One can be enfolded into the other in ways that enhance the benefits of both, yet they are not the same. Stillness is a state of wholeness, an antidote to the fragmentation of BIPOC people that comes with marginalization. "When we are fragmented, [we are] lost from ourselves, our culture, our people, our communities, the earth, our light, [our shadows and our darkness,] from God and our 'spiritness.'"[2] In the midst of crisis, there is fragmentation and wounding. Sitting in stillness may allow the pieces of us to reassemble. But sometimes, the crisis is so devastating that the healing requires drumming and song, chanting and ritual, not just once, but often. There is stillness in the midst of it all.

As it turns out, contemplation that arises from a crisis or collective trauma is a displacement of everyday life and a freefall into "what comes next." As the crisis sweeps away our former life together, our arrogance and fantasies, all we can do is reflect on the memories of another and a more tranquil existence, and accustom ourselves to a new and welcoming darkness.

The darkness to which I refer is not a space of fear. It is an involuntary centering in a reality that is not always available to us when our egos are lit. Crises open portals of a deeper knowing. When the crisis occurs, the only way out is through, so we take a cue from nature and relax into the stillness, depending upon one another and the breath of life![3]

Jesus as Liberator

By Richard Rohr

I N THE 1970S, I read Dominican author Robert Nolan's book called *Jesus Before Christianity* and realized that most of us had never met Jesus before Christianity. Both Catholics and Protestants had largely been presented with a "churchified" Jesus. Excellent Jesus scholarship over the last several decades has helped us to recognize that there was a certain grid at work that determined what we paid attention to in Jesus and what we largely ignored. We now have access to linguistic knowledge that helps us understand the most ancient manuscripts and also disciplines like anthropology, cultural studies, and more. We recognize the political and historical contexts in which Jesus says things in the Gospels—and until we appreciate that, we really miss the message.

In this article, I concentrate on four areas where I think Jesus was trying to liberate us from something.

W HAT WAS JESUS LIBERATING US FROM? This probably won't seem too different from what we would now call the ego or the false self. As Jesus put it, "Those who find their life will lose it, and those who lose their life for my sake will find it" (Matthew 10:39). Buddhists tend to describe this process with much greater clarity, but Jesus didn't have access to psychological language. He didn't need it. He just spoke in a straightforward way that his contemporaries could understand.

Scholarship today is discovering a much more radical and demanding Jesus than either Catholicism or Protestantism was ever ready for. We distorted the message so it wasn't primarily about a transformation from the ego but a transformation or freedom from the body self. We largely transferred everybody's guilt concerns toward the body. We concentrated on repressing and punishing the body, not giving the body too much pleasure, freedom, or delight—not that there aren't issues there. But the ego, in my opinion, has gotten away scot-free in the Western church. We allowed egos to get out of control while being quite anxious to appear celibate, abstemious, and not too greedy. Some Protestant denominations make such things their entire concern!

Christianity has largely paid little attention to the real things Jesus talked about. Instead, we tend to be preoccupied with things that Jesus never talked about.

But who else can reform Christianity except Jesus?

Jesus tells his followers that they should never have what we would call *dominative* power. He calls it "lording it over others": "You know that the rulers of the Gentiles lord it over them...but not so with you" (Matthew 20:25–26). How did Christians come to understand that exercising power over others is what religion is all about? There's no indication that Jesus ever intended there to be a head church office somewhere, with upper, middle, and lower management. I'm lower management, as a priest—and we expected the laity to be passive followers. This is contrary to what Jesus taught and expected. He clearly gives power to people by giving them an inner authority.

Liberation from the self is liberation from the world of forms, display, and images. His word for that was *mammon*: "You cannot serve God and mammon" (Matthew 6:24). If you're playing the game of appearance and power, prestige and possessions, Jesus says you cannot know God. That's pretty absolute! There is an almost complete correlation between our preoccupation with image and how much—or how little—we've experienced the inner life.

Jesus also liberates us from self in terms of constant warnings against negativity and oppositional thinking. In general, his word for that liberation is *forgiveness*. Two thirds of Jesus's teaching is directly or indirectly about forgiveness. To live oppositionally is to be holding some degree of resentment or unhealed negative energy that we have not brought to the divine presence for transformation.

LIBERATION FROM RELIGION

S ECONDLY, JESUS DID not just try to liberate people from themselves. His main work seems to be the liberation of religion. His harshest words are for religion and religious leaders. Read the latter parts of all four Gospels. They go out of their way to point out that it is the high priests and elders of the people who kill Jesus. It's not really about the Jews or Judaism. It's the religious establishment. Christians historically scapegoated Jews, with anti-Judaism and then Christian antisemitism, all while missing Jesus's larger critique of religion itself.

The heroes of all Jesus's stories are non-Jews. Jesus makes the Samaritans, Romans, and unbelievers the heroes of his stories, and he makes his fellow Jews the villains. He utterly criticizes his own religion, and yet today, in most of our denominations, there is little room for the self-criticism of the prophet. When religion does not have prophets, we basically reject the capacity for internal self-criticism. When any institution or group is no longer capable of internal self-criticism, it becomes idolatrous. It becomes self-serving, self-maintaining, self-perpetuating, and self-validating.

Jesus is highly critical of religious debt and purity codes. He even flaunts them. I've often said Jesus did all his work on Saturday—as provocation! He's always doing everything that he knows will upset his Jewish contemporaries. He's saying, "You've missed the point! The Sabbath is not really about not doing work. It's about resting in God. You're telling me I can't heal people on the Sabbath? I'm going to prove I can."

Jesus also does not validate ingroup thinking over outgroup thinking. Once we do that, we have laid the foundation for violence, just as we have with our obsession over power, prestige, and possessions. We have to under-cut power, prestige, possessions, and ingroup/outgroup thinking or we will always have a violent society.

Jesus was much more prophet than priest. He was a traveling sage, a wisdom teacher. He never claimed the word priest for himself—and it was the priests who killed him. You'd think we would go out of our way to *not* want to be priests and simply want to be servants, as he called his twelve disciples to be.

He almost universally taught a doctrine of love, mercy, and relationship over any kind of religious asceticism or dietary laws. But Jesus is accused of being a glutton and wine drinker because he doesn't go the ascetical route. I'm not saying that having some ascetical practices is wrong—but don't make too much of them. Otherwise, we make a god or religion out of our practices and preferences. We think we've achieved some kind of higher purity because we don't do this or don't touch that. Jesus has no use for that kind of religion. Purity and debt codes are low-level religion, which creates superiority systems.

Jesus is clearly much more concerned about healing now than salvation later. How did we miss this? Jesus goes where the suffering is. His starting place is human pain, not private sin. There are almost no prerequisites for any of Jesus's healings except *desire itself*. Those who desire healing receive healing. Jesus never asks people what denomination they belong to, if they are baptized, if their marriage was annulled, or what their sexual orientation is. Denying that you are a sinner is, for Jesus, much more dangerous than sin itself. He calls it the sin against the Holy Spirit, the inner witness (see Matthew 12:31–32). Thinking that you are better or holier than other people is the real problem.

There is no indication that Jesus taught dependency on outer authority as the way to become close to God. Jesus gave us the basis for a strong inner authority and inner experience. Our very simple word for that is *prayer*. If I stopped teaching on all other topics for a few years and just taught contem-plative prayer, we would all know this for ourselves.

LIBERATION FROM THE CONVENTIONAL
SOCIAL ORDER

THIRDLY, I THINK Jesus came to liberate us from the "conventional social order." By and large, Christianity makes us good citizens of the conventional social order. For example, Jesus idealizes the "big family" over the small, nuclear family. He idealizes the universal spiritual family, which he calls the reign of God.

He also never idealizes the ethnic or national family or patriotism. Americans are on bended knee before this piece of cloth called the American flag. We don't see that in the Scriptures. That's called idolatry. Worshipping any human creation or human boundaries was the major sin in the Hebrew Scriptures. American Christianity has come so far from the gospel that it is much more a religion of church and state. We Americans inherited it from Europeans and didn't even see the conflict with it. Only God is to be worshiped, not the flag of any country.

Jesus consistently teaches from the perspective of the lower class. Whereas the church has historically been preoccupied with maintaining class and creating class distinctions, Jesus constantly undercuts any concern for upward mobility or class status. "The last will be first, and the first will be last" is probably his most common one-liner (Matthew 20:16). Wouldn't you think, if that were true, we'd all be living like St. Francis of Assisi? Wouldn't you think we'd be trying to be as little, inconsequential, and poor as possible?

That surely hasn't been the story of Christian history. Capitalism has spiraled out of control in the so-called Christian countries—and we've exported it to the rest of the world. This again shows how little effect Jesus has had on us at the corporate, collective level. We make his message about individual sin and individual salvation, while neglecting to take his message to the corporate, systemic level. Jesus reveals and condemns the violence that will always proceed from these unquestioned games of power, prestige, and possessions.

FINALLY, JESUS CAME to liberate us from what I describe as "mind games." Did it ever strike you as unusual that Jesus put nothing in writing? Why didn't Jesus come later, in the time of the printing press? He tells stories and parables. He's not a systematic thinker or theologian. That's why systematic theology has not known how to quote him. If you're into philosophy and theology, you might have a hard time with Jesus. He's not going to lend himself to that game. He picks blue-collar workers as his leaders. Why didn't he go to Jerusalem and pick lawyers, scholars, or doctors of the law as followers? Instead, he picks fishermen and tax collectors.

He seems to prefer solitude and silence over study. He must have studied the Scriptures, but whenever he wants clarification, he spends time apart. He teaches simple religious practices over any major theorizing. Rome's preoccupation for the greater part of 1,000 years has focused on being a type of thought police for the world. But there's no indication Jesus wanted any of his followers to be thought police. The only thoughts Jesus told us to police were our own negative, violent, and hateful thoughts, not other people's thoughts. Where did Jesus say there was a set of mental abstractions we needed to believe that would make God love us or ensure we went to heaven?

Jesus teaches trust and acceptance over any control or predictability. But we want predictability, and we've grown used to control. It's normal for an institution to want predictability. I'm not naïve about institutionalization. I've had to learn in my years as a priest that I can be a part of it and even offer a certain degree of allegiance to it—but not too much, because my real life is not identified with it. I criticize Christianity by the values Christianity taught me. That's the paradox. Ironically, it's by being a consummate insider that I have the authority to talk this way. I'm an ordained priest who's been educated in the system—but I also understand why the system isn't everything.

Quite simply, Jesus came to liberate us for God.

I F WE DO THIS LIBERATION WORK, I'm convinced that we fall into the hands of the living God. Once the inflated ego, false religion, conventional thinking, and mind games are out of the way, we don't need techniques, methods, and formulas. Jesus is clearly a teacher of alternative, subversive wisdom. This level of wisdom at first shocks or even disappoints us. It takes away our comfort in conventional thinking. Most people have been raised to think the church is here to make us good citizens who obey all rules of social control and order. It never occurred to such people that the gospel was anything different from the state.

Many of us really think church and state are the same thing. We've been lapdogs of the empire. As our empire increasingly becomes a danger to the entire world, we must recover the true Jesus and the true gospel.

So, what did Jesus liberate us *for*? Quite simply, Jesus came to liberate us for God. You might think that's a cliché, but religion has been an obstacle course instead of a highway to God. It's been largely a worthiness contest. Jesus turns that on its head by idealizing the unworthy. Jesus is the most unlikely founder of a religion because he idealized those who weren't worthy: sinners, drunkards, and tax collectors. We should all be breathing a great sigh of relief. If you know you're a sinner, you're relieved by this message.

The little ones rejoice in Jesus, and the establishment fights Jesus. Those who have fought for their worthiness, who have attained their social and religious status by following debt and purity codes, live as if they have no need for grace, mercy, love, prayer, or forgiveness. Such people stand against the Holy Spirit or "inner witness." The word *witness* is used several times by Paul and John to describe the indwelling divine presence, the inner knower. There is within us a homing device that Jesus promised to leave with us. In the beginning of Acts 2, this Spirit falls on everyone, without any distinction of nationality, religion, race, or gender. Pentecost is the utter democratization of religion, the universalization of the gift. We just need some spiritual practices to make contact with that inner knower, the indwelling presence, the Holy Spirit.

The rediscovery of that inner guide is always the work of great religion. In John's Gospel, Jesus even uses a word from the legal system to describe this Holy Spirit: Paraclete. *Parakletos* is a Greek word for defense attorney. Jesus says, "I'm giving you a defense attorney because the human spirit is so beaten down and filled with self-doubt, self-hatred, and self-criticism." We think we're nothing, and Jesus says he will give us an inner knower who will fight on our side, defending us against the voices of negativity and oppression that demean or humiliate us. We must make contact with the inner witness, the inner knower, who knows we are a beloved child of God.

Whether we know it or not, this is the basis for the mystical life. We can all be mystics and saints now. It has nothing to do with moral achievement. Being moral hasn't gained us one ounce of time in heaven or grace from God. Jesus came to announce that God cannot be achieved. He called it the gospel, the "good news."

Jesus liberates us for God, for the integration of our humanity with our divinity, and for a friendly universe where we can rest. We don't need to fix anything or make it right. We don't even need to understand it. The word for that is *faith*. I can't prove the inner knower to you, but you can tell when someone has experienced the divine presence. It's like an energy field. People want to gather together, pray together, serve others together. They want to stop war together, reconcile opposites together.

Everywhere I go, I meet free, happy people who live by the Spirit, who want to love, who want to be kind, who want to change the world, who want to heal their neighbor, and who are not into killing, vengeance, and capital punishment. It's an evolved consciousness. Jesus liberates us for God, for the gospel, for others, and for the world.

Our liberation for others is a participatory life. We come to this by connecting—not by doing it right, but by being in right relationship. Our very image of God as Trinity is a perfect illustration of right relationship that does not exercise dominative power. If God in God's self is right relationship, then the mystery of church is right relationship, and the mystery of healing is right relationship. It's not about being right. It's about being rightly connected. Who we are is the sum of our relationships. This is why healing, forgiveness, letting go, and apology are so necessary.

I remember the first time I did a sweat lodge with Native Americans. After we came crawling out of the sweat lodge naked, we all put our heads to the Earth. We looked at the other brothers, and we said, "All my relations." It means that I'm reconnected. I'm realigned with everything. That's what Jesus means by the reign of God. He distinguishes that awareness and that level of connection from the politics of this world. Jesus seemed to believe that if enough people could connect at that level of communion, of consciousness, of transformation, and of love, that corporate power could change the world.

Jesus's Jewish tradition taught that God is saving history. His message wasn't an individualistic message. Jesus wants us to understand that God is liberating history, which has grown, as Paul put it, toward fullness, toward freedom, and toward salvation (see Ephesians 1:10). All of us as individuals are caught up in that universal sweep of God's love. Each of us is only a little part of this great big mystery. In our wholeness, in our right relationship, and in our communion with one another, we are the body of Christ.

Adapted from Richard Rohr, *Jesus as Liberator / Paul as Liberator*, audio series, (Center for Action and Contemplation, 2007).

Translatio Divina:

The Living Tradition of Translating Love into Life Practice

By Carmen Acevedo Butcher

Every single time you make the two one, and when you make the inside like the outside and the outside like the inside, and the sky above like the earth below,

...

and every time you make true eyes
in place of an eye,
and a true hand
in place of a hand,
and a true foot
in place of a foot,
and your true image
in place of your face,
then you will enter the kindom.

—word 22, the gospel of toma, translated by
Carmen Acevedo Butcher[1]

W ITH THE GIFT OF FIFTEEN THOUSAND SUNRISES, I've
lived among those with desert sand between their toes, literally
and metaphorically. They cherish kind community, care for the
poor, reverence the earth, pray unceasingly, and embody making-the-two-
one wisdom.

I've spent decades steeping in and translating into English the teachings
of these ancient, medieval, and early-modern Jesus mystics, like the words
above from my translation of the gospel of toma (the Gospel of Thomas).
My translation work has shown me that the path of loving transformation
is everywhere and accessible to all.

These ancestors' voices animate and nourish contemporary contemplative Christianity. In my *nous*, that nowhere where I most deeply listen,
a fourth-century desert monk is always praying, "δεόμεθα ποίησον ἡμᾶς
ζῶντας ἀνθρώπους," and I immerse myself in his Greek, translating, so we
may pray together: "We beg you, make us come alive as humans in community."[2] Engaging with this wisdom restores our vision, for in imitating
Christ, the desert *abbas, ammas,* and others often demonstrated "an amazing awareness of the connection between the one seeing and what is seen,"[3]
as Richard Rohr reflects.

Over a millennium later, Br. Lawrence (1614–1691) demonstrated this
awareness too. He made activities like flipping omelettes, stirring stews,
and mending sandals into unceasing prayer. As I translated his down-to-
earth teaching from French, the realization dawned that I'd been practicing the presence—talking–with–and–listening–to God—since childhood,

but grief-blinded. I'm thankful the friar gifted me this gold in my shadow. Br. Lawrence is also encouraging, like so many mystics I've translated. He says that focusing the mind solely on God is "the easiest" form of prayer, and he reassures a nun struggling with how hard contemplative habits can seem at first: "The mind is extremely likely to wander."[4] By practicing with "great faithfulness" to cultivate an inner awareness of God, eventually the friar lived into and from it, saying: "I no longer believe, but I see. I experience."[5]

My gratitude for him, and other Christian mystics, is deep. Translating their wisdom has translated my Self, returning me to Me.[6] This communion helped save my life. Their loving *nous* attuned my heart's ear to the ordinary goodness of listening to Silence and embraced my grief when I didn't even know I was grieving.

I was grieving the loss of my father to an undiagnosed disorder and my family to his recurring physical and verbal violence. For my childhood psyche, fragmented by this trauma, the loving wisdom of my mystic friends was balm. It began knitting me back together through intimate encounters simply called *translation*. These ancient psychologists stepped unafraid into my messy life with kindness, soul medicine, and practical exercises. Counseling also helped.

Before I could hold my own trauma, I held manuscripts and pondered their lacunae-obscured words, where losses to fire, water, sun, time, and inhumanity have made holes in parchment and vellum. A translator develops an eye for beholding these gaps with gentle, openhearted concern. This was helpful practice for witnessing my own pain.

Unsurprisingly, curricula vitae (CV) have lacunae too, by exclusion. CVs, as small ego paeans, praise Fulbrights or Phi Beta Kappas, but neglect suffering. I remember, though. During graduate school, I slept at most three hours a night. Getting out of bed felt like lifting an iron sheet off my chest. Years later, I understood I was one of "a great many [childhood trauma] survivors"[7] who suffered depression and chronic anxiety, as Judith Herman observes.

Lonely too, in my back pocket I'd tuck a three-by-five card with Scripture handwritten on it. On long walks, I'd pull it out to read, reflect, and respond. Tucking it back, letting the remembered words ride my strides, I'd eat them in this ancient way, as Jeremiah 15:16 says, "When I discovered your words, I devoured them; they became a source of joy to me." I met this habit young, when my mother handed me a slip on which she'd typed Philippians 4:13, saying, "Memorizing Bible verses helps me." Gradually, memorizing

An act of liberation, translation is at once personal and communal.

morphed into something I had no name for yet. Scripture-lit deep praying opened me to contemplation. Practicing was uphill at first, like Athens' steep streets, but I kept trying.

A full-time student, I was also teaching first-year composition full time, while living with undiagnosed dyslexia. Reading and writing were bone-wearying then. When my eye began twitching and wouldn't stop, I knelt beside my narrow bed in my one-bedroom apartment, my mind crackling like radio static. Feeling fractured, I prayed, "HELP ME PLEASE—I can't do it."

Then, in a random meeting with a professor, I met a calm Benedictine monk named Ælfric. It didn't matter that he'd died in England around 1014 CE. He was alive to me. His serene sermons on the Gospel of John kept saying, *Carmen, God loves you*. Ælfric also preached that giving to the poor is loving Christ: "If love isn't willing to work, then it isn't love."[8] He showed me that my gentle mother's active, embodied loving was my own path, not the heart-numbing pursuit of right belief preached in the churches of my childhood.

Translating Ælfric's tranquil poetic prose, hours daily, gave me infusions of peace. Through my dedication to him then, and by extension his monastic community, I experienced the entrainment usually associated with a physically embodied, healthy community. These living spirits made a container for me in which to see my Self. Their teaching revealed my own innate calm, that "true image" within, as word 22 sings.

This was all very gradual. The mystics' words regulated my painful, confusing emotions, returning me to Love, letting me taste the joy of *apatheia*, or inner peace. The writer bell hooks names love as our desperately needed freedom: "America is a culture of domination... The moment we choose to love we begin to move against domination... The moment we choose to love we begin to . . . act in ways that liberate ourselves and others."[9]

An act of liberation, translation is at once personal and communal. In a way, all contemplatives are translators. Moving aside to make room inside to let another take center stage, translators listen deeply to what another person is trying to communicate. In that way, translating is like spiritual direction/companionship, or good therapy, or friendship. Engaging in translation strengthens any mystic's—a.k.a., human's—empathy, which is a "necessary"[10] trait for translators, as Jhumpa Lahiri says.

Since translating spiritual texts has been for me a powerful form of *lectio divina* or sacred reading, I name it *translatio divina*—"sacred translating."[11] While translating *The Cloud of Unknowing* and sequel *The Book of Privy Counsel* from Middle English, I recognized parts of me I'd rejected. My new friend then, its author, Anonymous, an experienced contemplative and an empowering teacher, kept me company in my shadow work: "Keep on trying... because the more you learn, the more you can teach me."[12] Practice faithfully, he affirms: "You'll sense that God has become your teacher and that by God's grace these contemplative techniques have become second nature to you."[13]

Anonymous teaches that even our longing is praying: "You only need a naked intent towards God."[14] For those thinking they have no time to practice, he adds, "Some people believe contemplation is time-consuming, but it's not... It's as brief as an atom."[15] He recommends *lectio divina*—read, reflect, respond—as contemplation's ground.

During *lectio divina* and *translatio divina*, I experience deep, unrushed, intimate, repeated receiving-reflecting-responding-to Love, and resting in God or Ultimate Reality, as delicious, nourishing, and transforming. The mystics introduced me to self-compassion.

The tired soul resting in Silence sees with new eyes. Wonder quickens. We grow more curious. Little by little, as we practice, we are more mindful of the truth already there: *I am love, others are love, the earth and its more-than-human creatures are love, and I am meant to be love in this world, both to myself and to all others.*

Being bipedal miracles who run on cups of coffee, we need reminders of this reality.

Translating the gospel of toma reminded me anew that mystical truths help us release our binary default. I spent large sums of that one real currency, time, looking up its words in Coptic and Greek dictionaries, reading background sources, studying excellent scholars' ideas, rereading, exploring etymologies, and weighing the words' poetry against myriad scholarly interpretations. Cognizant that innumerable complex elucidations exist for each word (and lacuna), I translated to capture its wise poetic layers.

Now, whenever I'm in the kitchen washing dishes, word 22, seemingly impromptu, rises in my heart like the sun. I hear Jesus saying gently to me at the sink: *make the inside / like the outside and the outside / like the inside*. I slow my washing then, ensuring I mind the outside of the bowl and wash it as well as the inside, remembering they are one bowl. This tiny break reminds me that I love this simple bowl, in this moment, in this kitchen, with my family and cats nearby and every aspect of our messy lives together. And all of you.

Whenever I let my small ego go, I enter the anything-can-happen space of nondualism. Here lives compassion, for self and others. Beyond-dualism, as love's vernacular, gives me hope.

May we all be translators of, and translated by, this universal language.

Resting in
Darkness

By Douglas E. Christie

"T HIS IS THE DARK silence in which all the loving are lost."[1]
That is how the great medieval Flemish mystic John Ruusbroec
(1293–1381) described the culmination of the Christian spiritual
life: a descent into a dark silence or stillness where love and loss move
together, where we are held in darkness *by* love, where loss and darkness
become the very climate in which we come to know ourselves as beloved.

The mind strains to take in this paradoxical vision: Darkness, at least
the way we often experience or imagine it, hardly seems hospitable to the
experience of love. The night is so often a place where those unnamable
fears and anxieties that haunt our dreams emerge with all their disturbing
force, undermining our capacity to believe or live in love. So too with loss,
which in its most intense expressions can feel like a crippling absence that

undoes all possibility of meaning and hope. How can love even exist in such bleak, empty places? How can we renew our own capacity for love amidst such deep loss and unknowing?

These questions, which come to us so often in the depth of the night, are also well known to Christian contemplatives, mystics, and poets. And while we often look to them to help guide us into the light, they can also be immensely helpful to us as we struggle to navigate the darkness that so often haunts our lives. So many of these writers are at home in the darkness, attentive to its importance in their quest for God, aware of how darkness and unknowing can lead us deep into the mystery of our lives and the life of God. This is especially true in moments characterized by what Carmelite writer Constance Fitzgerald calls a sense of "impasse," when all known markers of meaning and direction suddenly disappear, and we find ourselves wandering in an unknown landscape, far from home, deeply uncertain about who we are, where we are, or where we are going.

In the opening canto of his *Divine Comedy*, the poet Dante Alighieri (1265–1321) described this lostness with an uncommon depth of feeling:

> Midway in our life's journey, I went astray
> from the straight road and woke to find myself
> alone in a dark wood.[2]
>
> Death could scarce be more bitter than that place!

Alone in a dark wood. This is where the journey so often begins: in a bitter, dark, difficult place, where the way ahead (if there is one at all) is unknown, inaccessible. Nor does the poet do anything to soften the sense of loneliness and emptiness of this experience. All he can do, it seems, is begin walking, wandering along a path whose destination is unknown to him.

Such experience was not uncommon for Christian contemplatives and mystics. The thirteenth-century Flemish mystic Hadewijch of Antwerp wrote: "I wander in darkness without clarity, without liberating consolation, and in strange fear," evoking the immense cost of becoming vulnerable to the power of *Minne* or love, which calls us endlessly forward, into the depths.[3] "We sail on in darkness,"[4] says Amma Syncletica, one of the early

The Christian mystical tradition reminds us again and again that the experience of loss and unknowing cannot be avoided.

desert mothers—a reminder of how old and persistent these concerns are and how necessary it was in certain moments of the spiritual journey to enter the depths of the night.

So it is with us. We grapple often with what W. G. Sebald (1944–2001) called: "Night, the astonishing, the stranger to all that is human."[5] We encounter a darkness that sometimes brings the end of something in ourselves, a Joban sense of displacement that is opaque, unknowable, endless.

One recent moment, shared by many across the world, stands out in my memory. On March 27, 2020, as the full weight of the COVID-19 pandemic was descending upon us, Pope Francis (1936–2025) stood alone in St. Peter's Square and expressed something that many of us were just beginning to feel: "For weeks [months] now, it has been evening. Thick darkness has gathered over our squares, our streets, and our cities. It has taken over our lives... We find ourselves afraid. And lost."[6] We lived for a long time in that darkness. Even after the pandemic abated, other sources of fear and uncertainty have arisen to haunt us. "Sometimes," wrote poet Alejandra Pizarnik (1936–1972), "we suffer too much reality in the space of a single night."[7]

Is darkness mostly about loss and unknowing, a reminder of the bleakness and dread at the heart of human experience? Or can we also affirm, with teachers in the Christian mystical tradition, that it can tell us something important about who we hope to become in our lives, what it means to open ourselves to God and one another in love? Can we learn, as the anonymous author of the fourteenth-century *Cloud of Unknowing* counsels us to do, to "rest in darkness"? Can we enter the silence and stillness at the heart of contemplative prayer and discover there a love nourished in darkness, a *deeply shared* love that Ruusbroec and many other Christian mystics refer to simply as "the common life"?

The Christian mystical tradition reminds us again and again that the experience of loss and unknowing cannot be avoided—and that sometimes the meaning of such experience eludes us. But it is also insistent that we are always held in God—Julian of Norwich (c. 1343–1416) wrote that God "enwraps us and enfolds us, embraces us and wholly encloses us, surrounding us out of tender love, so that he can never leave us."[8]

We cannot always say why or how we find ourselves drawn toward "the dark silence in which all the loving are lost," or how we can open ourselves to this journey into the depths and begin to discover (again) who we are most deeply in God. But it is important to remain attentive to those unexpected moments when darkness and unknowing overtake us.

A moment that had particular importance for me occurred during the summer of 2013, when I moved with my family to Córdoba, Argentina. An unexpected invitation had come to my wife and me to help establish an immersive study-abroad program there, based on the Jesuit ideal of "education for solidarity." At first, the invitation unsettled us. Were we the right people to do this work? Should we uproot our family and move six thousand miles away, to a radically different place and culture? Could we actually do it?

Eventually, we decided to accept the invitation and soon found ourselves traveling into the depths of the Southern cone, along with four of our five children and our cat, to begin a new life. We had a sense of trust that we were being called into this work, but very little clarity about what it would actually mean to respond and live into that call.

This sense of unknowing only deepened during our time in Argentina, especially that first year, when almost every aspect of our life brought us face to face with how little we knew or understood. It was not only the language or our lack of familiarity with the city where we found ourselves living. Nor was it simply the challenge of learning all the rudiments of daily living—how to pay our electric bill, how much to tip the *remis* driver, when to befriend and when to avoid the feral dogs that moved through the city in joyous and unpredictable packs, how to participate in the intricate and ever-present national ritual of sharing *mate* with friends and strangers, learning how differently *time* worked here and how little value seemed to be given to using time efficiently, and how much delight there was to be found in improvising, in walking a path with no known destination.

Gradually, we began to recognize that we were moving within a world where the very ideas of plans and control were often swept away in favor of a continuous, unpredictable unfolding of life—which was almost never on our terms or according to our ideas. We were being invited into a daily, moment-by-moment practice of relinquishment, of openness to whatever might happen next, something we noticed was far less difficult for our Argentine friends than it was for those of us from North America: the stripping away of expectations, the acceptance of all that could not be known, the embrace of life and community in the present moment.

"Nobody knows anything." These words from the *Sayings of the Desert Fathers* came back to me during our early days in Córdoba. I had encountered this saying years before, and I remember being baffled and amused by it. Really? Nobody knows *anything*? Even in a tradition of spiritual practice that places so much trust in the open, empty space of silence and stillness, this seemed excessive. Now, I read it differently: as a consoling word, an invitation to accept and embrace what Pseudo-Dionysius called *agnosia* or "unknowingness." This is an attitude or disposition born of a recognition of the vast field of mystery in which we find ourselves moving, a healthy skepticism about trusting too much in our limited knowledge of things, a refusal to imagine that we can manage or control everything that happens to us, and a willingness to face and open ourselves to what Simon Ortiz calls "the vastness beyond ourselves."[9]

We were *extranjeros*. In truth, we knew hardly anything about where we were or what to do. Often, we felt helpless. Still, we were welcomed by our friends and neighbors into this new place with such profound hospitality, carried along by the immense kindness shown to us by those with whom we lived and worked, and blessed by the deep warmth and joy that suffused Cordobése life and culture.

Slowly, we came to feel our helplessness to be a kind of gift. We had to start again at the beginning, like children, and learn the rudiments of the language, culture, and social reality of this place. It was painful and at times humbling. But it was good for us. It helped us to let go of many of the habits of autonomy and self-sufficiency that had become second nature to us in the United States and to begin recovering a sense of openness to a reality that far exceeded our capacity to understand or control. This, in turn, made it possible for us to open ourselves to a simple giving and receiving of love. We were so deeply *dependent* upon others, and from this simple dependence emerged a beautiful and vibrant experience of community.

Some of what I am describing will perhaps feel familiar or even obvious: the shift in orientation and self-perception that comes when we relinquish our place at the center of things and allow ourselves to be taken up as part of a whole. It can happen almost anywhere and in any circumstances. Still, in my experience, such relinquishment does not come easily. The loss of ground that makes this possible often comes upon us unawares, through circumstances not of our own making. We suddenly realize we are lost and that finding our way back from or through this loss is not entirely up to us.

We begin inhabiting this new place of unknowing, initially because we have no choice, but eventually with greater acceptance, trust, and vulnerability. We find ourselves looking out onto the world from there with new questions that would never have occurred to us within a place of relative comfort and security—especially the question of how to inhabit darkness and unknowing as part of our own spiritual practice.

Traditions of contemplative thought and practice—in particular, apophatic traditions rooted in darkness and unknowing that invite a radical relinquishment for the sake of a deeper and more abiding encounter with God—can help us with this work, especially through their careful reflection on what it means to honor the unknowability and ineffability of spiritual experience. The medieval French Beguine and mystic Marguerite Porete (1250–1310) wrote: "God is none other than the One of whom one can understand nothing perfectly... about whom one does not know how to say a word."[10] Still, in that deep silence, we can sometimes find ourselves drawn ever more deeply into what Thomas Merton (1915–1968) called "the hidden ground of love."[11]

How are we then to proceed? The consistent counsel of those who have traveled this path before us is this: pay attention, listen, remain open, let silence gather and deepen. Allow yourself to be taken up into "the dark silence in which all the loving are lost." Notice who is present with you in that space. Open yourself to the power and beauty of the common life. Rest in darkness.

The Integration of Shadow

By Elise Loehnen

I THINK EVERYONE WHO HAS WORKED WITH ME has really liked me," I suggested, peering at my friend over my chopped salad.

She laughed so hard in response I worried she might choke on a neatly cubed piece of cucumber.

"What's the joke? Why is that so funny?"

"Oh honey," she replied. "Do you really believe that?"

I nodded, now fully confused.

"I can promise you that some people didn't like you and continue to not like you. You're not for everyone—and guess what? Nobody is. That's a wild thing to believe! I'm sure there are people saying things about you that would make you want to curl up and die—and that's life, honey. Do *you* like everyone?"

This woman sitting across from me is one of my mentors. She's wise, seasoned, and tough—and she has a lot of affection for the unvarnished truth. Sometimes, to quote Richard Schwartz, PhD, the creator of Internal Family Systems therapy, she's one of my *tor*-mentors, there to hold up a mirror and show me bits of myself that I'm not always pleased to see.

After lunch, I thought about what she had said—and to her point, how absurd it is to stake one's identity on appealing to everyone, on making palatability the goal. At forty-five, you'd think I would understand that, to paraphrase Epictetus, you can't control the world, only the way you respond to the world. By the same token, you can't control other people and how they might feel about you.

But still, I couldn't get comfortable. The prospect of displeasing anyone felt deeply unnerving. Was I not as universally beloved as I wanted to believe? Did people think I was mean, or rude, or dismissive, or... *toxic*? Did they say these things about me?

As I sat with that possibility, my mind spinning, I felt a familiar swell of anxiety: mounting tightness in my chest, shortening exhales—a fear response. After all, one of the most damaging, most threatening things that you can do to a woman in our culture is reputational harm—to say that she's a bad mother, a toxic boss, an inattentive or selfish coworker or friend. Women will "disappear" themselves when these assaults on their goodness come: Cue every celebrity takedown, the removal of female founders, and so on.

What's particularly pernicious is that women are not only trained to police ourselves. We're also trained to police each other. Our culture is a graveyard of women's reputations—and we are our own gravediggers. This is why, as a somewhat public writer, I felt like an appropriate target. Someone could bring me to my knees on social media by saying they thought I was a bad person. Nobody was attacking me, and yet there I was, alone in my car, feeling an instinct to defend myself rise, to use my "goodness" as a shield against even the *idea* that someone, somewhere, might dislike me. The fear that this idea could "get out there" and take root felt ruinous, ridiculously existential.

I recognized this pattern. I had been here before. I wrote an entire book about variations and flavors of this and the way our patriarchal culture conditions women for "goodness" and men for power. (Men can pretty much do *anything* that's grievous and harmful—so long as we perceive them as powerful. The worst thing you can say about a man, it seems, is that he's feminine, or weak.) I put "goodness" in quotes because I'm not talking about an internal or gnostic idea of goodness—the goodness that's baked into each of us.

I'm talking about the kind of goodness that's externally mediated and adjudicated, and made invisible by cultural norms. *This is the way things are. This is how it's always been.*

Does this sound *familiar*? A good woman is never tired. A good woman doesn't really want anything for herself—she's happy to subjugate everything she wants to other people's needs. Speaking of needs, a good woman needs no attention, affirmation, or praise. A good woman has no appetite. In fact, she has unswerving discipline for keeping her body small, under control, and compliant. A good woman doesn't talk about money (it's base and unspiritual!), yet keeps the general economy humming and her own budget tightly constrained. A good woman is desirable but never desiring, sexy but not sexual. And a good woman is never upset—furious or depressed—about any of this.

This punch card of performed "goodness" aligns with the Seven Deadly Sins: sloth, envy, pride, gluttony, greed, lust, and wrath. If you're rushing to your copy of the New Testament to fact-check me, don't bother: The sins don't appear in the Bible. They were first written down in the Egyptian desert by a monk named Evagrius Ponticus (345–399), who is also credited as an early father of the Enneagram. They were described as Eight Demonic Thoughts—distractions which would keep one out of prayer—and the eighth was sadness. Ponticus organized bits of scripture to use against these basic human instincts and desires, and this chapbook of prayer made its way through the desert.

In 590 CE, Pope Gregory I gave a fateful homily. In the New Testament, Mary Magdalene is described as the one from whom Jesus cast seven demons. In this homily, Pope Gregory I described the Seven Cardinal Vices—Evagrius Ponticus's list, minus sadness—and assigned them all to Mary Magdalene, conflating her with the one who anointed Jesus's feet with her hair and turning the two of them into a lone penitent prostitute. In this moment, the most prominent woman in the New Testament—aside from Mother Mary—became the repository for all sin. She wore this reputation until the papacy attempted to clear her name in the 1980s. (In 2016, Pope Francis made Mary Magdalene the Apostle to the Apostles, though some might argue that she was really the First Apostle, not Peter. After all, the resurrected Christ appeared first to her and gave her his first teaching.)

Before that lunchtime conversation, I had written a book about the collective cultural shadow of women. I had named everything that we've been conditioned to label as "bad," "deviant," and a threat to our status as "good women": sexual appetite; eating without restraint; wanting power, money, affirmation, and praise; and enjoying rest. But these natural human urges don't go "elsewhere" when we disavow them. We simply repress and suppress them in our bodies and then ultimately project them onto other people. We tend to shame other women for all the qualities and behaviors we refuse to own in ourselves. Even though they're still a part of us, we refuse to recognize them.

The poet Robert Bly (1926–2021) managed to encapsulate this perfectly, describing in *A Little Book on Human Shadow* how our shadow functions like a psychic trash bag, which we sling over our shoulders and haul around: "We spend our life until we're twenty deciding which parts of ourselves to put in the bag, and we spend the rest of our lives trying to get them out again."[1] While I kept filling my big black Hefty until I was forty, I did years of shadow work while writing my first book, extracting all the parts of myself that I had denied. As I came to understand through my lunchtime conversation with my *tormenter*, though, so much work remained ahead.

This is the slippery part of shadow work: We can't "see" what's in our shadow, because, by its very definition, it's in the dark. The term *shadow* comes from Swiss psychiatrist Carl Jung (1875–1961), who argued that the ego assumes the traits it wants and likes—often traits prioritized by culture—and relegates everything else to the "shadow" of the unconscious. My therapist, himself a Jungian, doesn't like the word *shadow* because of its associations with race, so he calls the shadow a blind spot, one that doggedly chases you through life, holding what you refuse to look at outside of conscious awareness. Your shadow, or blind spot, contains all the qualities that are a threat to your identity, or belief structures, or the parts of your psyche that you need to disavow and disown to self-protect.

For me, being perceived as unkind and therefore unlikable had not been something I could look at. It was too scary, particularly in our quick-to-cancel online world, so I told myself it was an impossibility. And to keep it as far away from me as possible, I spent a lot of energy trying to control people's perceptions of me, which at times meant performing patience and kindness I didn't feel or holding my tongue to conceal what I really thought—except, of course, for all the times when I forgot, or was misread, or let myself show up fully, without (self-) consciously holding myself back.

Because here's the thing about shadow: While we can't see our own, we can see everyone else's. How often do you find yourself on the road, cursing out another driver for cutting you off, only to do the same thing a few miles later, justifying your action to yourself because you're in a hurry or you're the better driver? It's a silly example, but it's shadow in action: We hate in others what we refuse to accept in ourselves. Meanwhile, anyone watching you

Our shadow functions like a psychic trash bag, which we sling over our shoulders and haul around.

drive from the passenger seat will chuckle at your hypocrisy. After all, didn't Jesus say, "Why do you see the speck in your neighbor's eye, but do not notice the log in your own eye?" (Matthew 7:3–5) Recognizing the log is hard, in part because we've been conditioned to believe that the log is bad and undesirable. We don't want to accept that these qualities and behaviors are in us too.

We live in a universe constructed through separation—of light from dark (Biblically), of the identities to which we belong versus those that we exclude or exclude us (practically). We are built and conditioned to see the world through these binaries. Our basic survival instinct is to codify people, places, things, and experiences as friendly or hostile, good or bad, right or wrong. Then we align our own psychology toward those values we esteem, values largely dictated by what our culture deems is correct. We do this automatically and unconsciously, in a search for safety and security. Our desire to belong, and to be on the winning team, is so strong that we're driven to perform our virtue publicly, to profess to the world all the ways we're on the "right" side of history or a person of ideal qualities. Meanwhile, we all find the effort exhausting—and also not an actual reflection of who we are. It takes a lot of energy to project—and then defend—a perfect image.

The beauty of shadow work is that once you can start to see your blind spots, you can integrate them. You can fill them with the light of awareness and thereby lighten your load. One wise teacher told me that shadow is simply space waiting to be filled with light, that it's a pacesetter on human evolution. Darkness is the fuel, material that must be metabolized and alchemized for growth. You can recognize "darkness" as something that feels other or unacceptable, yet this darkness belongs to all of us. Metabolizing your darkness leads you to a higher ground of acceptance—both for yourself and other people.

This takes conscious engagement though, because our instinct is to stand against and opposite what we want to disown. My office popularity example proves this point in a low-stakes way: So fearful of being labeled as bad, mean, or not nice, I insisted to the world that "Everybody likes me, I'm always kind," and clung to it. Threats to this identity felt—ridiculously—existential.

The reality of how people apprehend me is of course more nuanced and complex, as it is for everyone, in every situation. Now that I'm aware of it, I'm working to relax into this middle space, to accept that I don't need to be for everyone and to stop spending so much energy defending an impossible position in my head. There is a lot more spaciousness and room in the middle. There is grace.

We can do our shadow work in community too. I've come to understand through my work with women, for example, that when we recognize our shared history and inheritance, we can create the distance to start to reclaim those parts of us that we've sent into exile. As we make the cultural load conscious—as we see that when we project qualities on other people or groups, they're likely our own—it becomes less scary to sift through our own bag of shadowy "bad parts" and reclaim them as part of who we are. As Carl Jung is credited as saying, "I'd rather be whole than good."

The path to wholeness requires the integration of shadow. There's a lot more space and grace in allowing ourselves to be whole—to be good *and* bad, right *and* wrong, kind *and* mean, ugly *and* beautiful, somewhere between old *and* young—because *the spectrum is the reality*. We are all these things. It's only in our minds that we refuse to see and accept the truth, that we spend so much energy defending against what we don't want to accept about ourselves.

Doing shadow work requires skill, commitment, and ease with discomfort. As the world speeds up and becomes both more complex and more forceful in confronting us with its complexity, we need increased tolerance for managing our darker parts, in part so we don't consign others to carry our share of the shadow by projecting what we refuse to own onto them. We need tools for managing shadow-spiked uneasiness and for pulling ourselves out of binary thinking, where we try to assign "good" and "bad," placing ourselves always on the good team, where we can feel comfortable and righteous.

I believe we'd be better off if we can expand our view of who we really are, to work with reality and include the darker bits. To do this, we need to metabolize our part of the collective burden—and do our best to not add to it.

Standing at the Threshold:

Liminality, Illness, and Transformation

By Christine Valters Paintner

T HE MEDIEVAL WOMEN MYSTICS have fascinated me since my time studying Christian spirituality in graduate school over twenty years ago. Hildegard of Bingen (1098–1179) seized my imagination first: a mystic and visionary, writer and composer, preacher and healer, she was one example of a powerful woman who was able to subvert the patriarchal hold on religion and whose voice had spiritual authority. Teresa of Ávila (1515–1582) was a great reformer who lived during the time of the Inquisition. Margery Kempe (1373–1438) followed an inner call to go on pilgrimages to the Holy Land and the Camino de Compostela, while also being accused of heresy more than once. It is said Clare of Assisi (1194–1253) was able to avert a siege of Assisi by standing in her power, companioned by the Eucharist. Julian of Norwich (c.1343–after 1416) lived during a time when the Black Death killed almost half the population, and she shared visions of a God whose desire and foundation is only Love.

These women also experienced a variety of illnesses and chronic pain, some throughout their lives. One thing mysticism, spiritual visions, and illness have in common is a profound experience of life's liminality and call to dwell on the thresholds between worlds. The mystic is one who lives at the juncture between heaven and earth and lifts up all the ways they see the world-behind-the-world breaking through. The visionary is inspired by images that appear like dreams to instruct and inspire us about how we are to live fully in loving relationship with the divine presence.

LIMINALITY AND THE HORIZONTAL PERSPECTIVE

FROM MY OWN ONGOING EXPERIENCE with chronic illness, I like to describe the horizontal perspective we receive when forced to rest and lie in bed more hours than we would otherwise prefer. The world looks very different from a prone position, more vulnerable, more attuned to the needs of the body than the vertical perspective so prized by our modern culture.

In Dr. Terrill Gibson's beautiful book *The Liminal and the Luminescent*, he describes the power and necessity of making ourselves available to this liminal realm. The liminal is

> where our Destiny—both collective and individual—is revealed. Many believe that this in-between liminal realm, this vast, ripe emptiness within our understandings of conventional time and space, is where our primal wound is healed by the only ultimate balm there is—relationship and love... So, it is necessary to find the doorway, the portal, into such depth chambers of the psyche in order for such repeated, transformative exposure to occur. It is through this portal that the depth psycho-spiritual journey begins.[1]

This is the realm that the mystics regularly encounter and spend time. It is the place where we, as spiritual seekers, draw our inspiration, renewal, and healing. Rather than imagine the liminal as a space up in heaven, we might see it as a deep well within that we can draw upon through dreams and intuition, through opening our hearts to the gifts the Beloved offers to us, moment by moment. The portal to these healing waters is everywhere. All that is required is an opening of our eyes and our hearts, a quiet presence and attunement.

Another way we can access the veil between worlds is through any experience which humbles us, brings us to our knees, undoes us, or disorients us. Often, this comes through illness or some other kind of loss. When we are overcome by grief and suffering, if we can stay present to what is happening with us and not run away, Dr. Gibson tells us "we have an encounter with the Divine which brings freshness, renewal, and integration. Then we can ascend again but are now humbler, more grateful for life, with a keener eye on what is essential in our lives, and greater compassion for others."[2]

These virtues of humility, gratitude, and compassion are essential for our own personal and collective transformation. The medieval women mystics knew what it meant to suffer, and rather than be victimized by it, they allowed themselves to be transformed. These visionaries tell us again and again that the Beloved is always pouring out divine compassion and grace that we have knit into our being a deep hunger to receive. These mystics sat in the tension between the horrors of the world and its beauty with depth and consciousness and then offered the wisdom they gained back to their communities and to us across time.

THE MEDIAL ONE

MYSTICS AND VISIONARIES receive their insight and images from waking dreams, voices, and bodily sensations that often overcome them in the moment. Toni Wolff (1888–1953), who was Carl Jung's colleague, first called this way of knowing "medial." She described the one with access to the medial as one who stands in the liminal realm, receiving visions for personal and collective healing.

While Wolff calls this archetype the "medial woman," I prefer to change it slightly to the "Medial One" to honor and acknowledge that persons of all genders have this experience available to them. Jesus himself was a Medial One who stood on the edges of life, choosing to be with those who were rejected by society. His crucifixion, something many of these medieval women mystics prayed with, was the doorway between life and death.

Roberta Bassett Corson, a depth psychologist and clergywoman, writes in *Stepping Out of the Shadows: Naming and Claiming the Medial Woman Today* about two different ways of seeing the world:

> There is a great difference between *looking-at* and *seeing-through*. The ability to see-through is what primarily distinguishes medial women from others, and all her other qualities follow from this. In the process of seeing-through, the medial woman learns what to look for and how to behold what she sees with imaginative eyes. Through this practice the medial woman brings forth visions that cannot be seen when merely looking *at* something.[3]

The Medial One mediates their visions to the world. They stand with one foot in the earthly, tangible realm and one in the transcendent, holding the tension between the two. They are called to steward these messages from the divine presence which upend our assumptions about what makes life meaningful and what is of value. These messages are just tiny glimpses into the magnificent expanse that is the world shimmering behind the veil. They trust deeply in the mysterious nature of the liminal to be able to stay present there through discomfort and disorientation. They speak the language of the holy mysteries and help connect us to the ground of Love in a world that often feels cruel and deeply unjust.

Day and night dreams, creative art expression, pilgrimage, and connection to the natural world all seem to be primary languages of the Medial One. Doorways and other portals are the openings, access points in the landscape and in our hearts.

If you are on a spiritual path, seeking to connect to the Divine through prayer and practice, through human and nature connection, and wanting to bring that wisdom and aliveness back to your community as gift, you are a Medial One too.

The medieval women visionaries were committed to moving from the depths of prayer into prayerful action in the world. They stood with the dying at their own thresholds. They were with the lepers, those who stood on the edges of society. Their visions were not an exemption from the demands of a suffering world, but an invitation to see their action in partnership with the Beloved.

ILLNESS AS INITIATION

AS SOMEONE WHOSE ENTIRE ADULTHOOD has been marked by chronic illness, I became entranced when I discovered that many of the medieval women mystics also dealt with their own experiences of serious illness. Hildegard of Bingen is thought to have suffered from migraines, Clare of Assisi possibly from multiple sclerosis, Julian of Norwich was brought to the brink of death from illness, and Margery Kempe experienced postpartum psychosis, among many others.

While there are many portals to the liminal realm, illness remains one of the most powerful because of the way we are brought to profound vulnerability. I want to make clear that there is a significant difference between saying that my own lifelong struggle with rheumatoid arthritis was intended by God to teach me something and the far more humble and truthful perspective that my wrestling with illness, pain, and fatigue have revealed to me depths of meaning, compassion, and wisdom. I do not believe that we are ever "given" our illnesses to teach us lessons. A God who would do that is not a God I want to be in loving relationship with. But I do want to be in intimate connection with the Beloved who stays with me through the pain and helps me to bear it, to cultivate endurance and patience, and who ultimately helps transform the wounds into gift and grace.

There are many for whom pain obliterates their sense of self and they will never find meaning or grace in it. Whatever stories we tell about the divine presence need to make room for these stories as well.

I think we need more than theodicy (exploring why there is evil or pain in the world). We need examples of spiritual practices that can help us sustain our faith in the midst of pain and suffering. We need examples of others who have been able to cultivate patience and endurance.

Disability theologian Sharon Betcher explains in her powerful book *Spirit and the Politics of Disablement*, "we are, as a culture, experiencing massive levels of chronic pain. And we no longer have the religious or cultural know-how to tap into or open out such pain for social analysis, we no longer know how to use it as a motivational force of either personal or sociocultural change."[4]

In our modern medical model, eradicating pain is the goal, but we lose sight of the value that can come from approaching pain from a spiritual perspective as well. How can we live meaningful lives that encompass the pain we experience? How can our bodies reveal wisdom about living with deeper compassion for ourselves and others?

Betcher believes we might find rich models among the women mystics: "One does not overcome illness," she writes. "One lives with it like an ascetic, assuming it as a practice through which one might learn to cull out reactive forces and numbing habits, while staying present to being alive."[5]

Initiation is an experience of moving from one stage of life to another with deepened awareness and wisdom. Illness and other kinds of suffering can become initiatory when we approach these experiences not just as something we want to eliminate, but as a potential portal into the liminal realm. The central symbol of Christian faith is someone who went willingly to the place of profound physical pain, suffering, and ultimately death, passing through a portal of transformation. For many of these mystics, Christ becomes a partner in their pain and a teacher of compassion.

We are often afraid of our pain and suffering because they point to our fragility, and yet the modern philosopher and mystic Simone Weil (1909–1943) wrote that "the vulnerability of precious things is beautiful because it is a mark of existence."[6] Our bodily vulnerability and mortality are sometimes terrifying aspects of being human and alive, yet they also open the door to more intense living. Many of the ancient monks believed that daily contemplation of death was necessary for a deeper relationship with life.

This is how pain is transformed: by being witnessed and held.

To bear our illness with patient endurance is to stand in resistance to a culture that worships youth and health and demands our perpetual productivity to be valued. It means we resist glib explanations for why pain exists. Pain will inevitably visit us all in some form. Pain can steal our energy, our time, our relationships, and our sense of ourselves and our futures. We are called into loving presence with one another in the midst of the suffering we each experience. This is how pain is transformed: by being witnessed and held.

When we approach illness with humility and without triteness of explanation, when we open to the desire of the Beloved to be present to us in our suffering, when we open our hearts to what we might be invited to learn and what wisdom is awaiting us, we can be initiated through illness. Our horizontal perspective can open a doorway to the Holy One, seen from the perspective of humility and grace. We can move from being victims of our circumstances into compassionate and wise guides for others.

The Twelve
Steps as a
Mystical Itinerary

By Kristin Vieira Coleman

T HE CHRISTIAN MYSTICAL TRADITION is rich with allegories
of the soul's journey into union with God. This path traditionally
involves an awakening to our deep need for the Divine, followed
by conversion—a turning away from destructive patterns, and finally, a life
rooted in contemplation, in which we become increasingly aware of God's
boundless love. Classic mystical roadmaps such as Teresa of Ávila's *Interior
Castle*, John of the Cross's *Ascent of Mount Carmel*, and Bernard of Clairvaux's *Twelve Steps of Pride and Humility* chart this terrain.

In our time, contemplative teachers such as Fr. Richard Rohr, James Finley, and Fr. Thomas Keating have recognized the Twelve Steps of Alcoholics Anonymous as a modern expression of this tradition. Though not affiliated with any organized religion or institution, the Twelve Steps offer a simple yet profound framework for spiritual transformation—one that has guided millions into a deeper experience of humility, healing, and compassionate service.

The metaphor of spiritual journeying has deep biblical roots. In Genesis, Adam and Eve's disobedience results in their expulsion from Eden, initiating humanity's long exile from union with God. The stories of Abraham's wandering, the Israelites' exodus from Egypt, and the Jews' return from Babylonian captivity became powerful symbols of the soul's pilgrimage toward divine reunion. As Boyd Taylor Coolman writes, "Christian accounts of spiritual itinerancy...all assume a primal break in the ideal relationship between humanity and God, and a subsequent displacement or dislocation... the overcoming of which is the raison d'être for the spiritual journey."[1]

Early Christian mystics such as Origen of Alexandria, Gregory of Nyssa, and Pseudo-Dionysius used these biblical patterns to systematize the soul's ascent into God. Later mystics continued this tradition, especially in the medieval period. While their models vary, most include three interwoven stages: purgation (cleansing from sin), illumination (enlightenment and right living), and union (intimate communion with God). Though they may not emphasize social action in these stages, they consistently affirm that mystical union overflows into love of neighbor. Echoing the thought of Bernard of Clairvaux (1090–1153), "The soul, when it loves purely ... returns to others out of the abundance it has received."[2]

At first glance, addiction may seem far removed from the concept of a sacred journey. Its chaos and destruction appear primarily physical or psychological. But Alcoholics Anonymous insists that the problem is spiritual at its core: "We have been not only mentally and physically ill; we have been spiritually sick."[3] The Twelve Steps mention the problem of addiction only once—in Step One. The remaining steps focus on healing relationships with God, self, and others, culminating in a life of service. When read through the lens of Christian mysticism, the Twelve Steps align remarkably with the traditional stages of purgation, illumination, and union.

PURGATION

IN CLASSICAL MYSTICAL TEXTS, purgation refers to a process of moral purification—a turning from pride, greed, lust, and other vices toward divine friendship. It is not punishment, but preparation for deeper communion. As Gregory of Nyssa (c. 335–c. 394) wrote in *The Life of Moses*, "This is true perfection: not to avoid a wicked life because like slaves we servilely fear punishment...but to regard falling from God's friendship as the only thing dreadful."[4]

The Twelve Steps begin with a similarly humbling descent:

- *Step One*: We admitted we were powerless over alcohol—that our lives had become unmanageable.

- *Step Two*: Came to believe that a Power greater than ourselves could restore us to sanity.

- *Step Three*: Made a decision to turn our will and our lives over to the care of God as we understood Him.

Even for those who do not struggle with substance abuse, these steps name a universal truth: We are not in control. As Dr. Anna Lembke writes, "Addiction occurs on a spectrum. Most of us are not dealing with life-threatening addictions, but nearly all of us are struggling with some form of compulsive overconsumption."[5]

The spiritual journey begins not with what is right about us, but with an honest confrontation with what is broken. "God seems to have hidden holiness and wholeness in a secret place where only the humble will find it," Richard Rohr observes.[6] Step One is not despair—it is liberation. It allows us to drop the mask of control and admit our need for help.

Steps Four through Seven deepen this purgative process:

- *Step Four*: Made a searching and fearless moral inventory of ourselves.

- *Step Five*: Admitted to God, to ourselves, and to another human being the exact nature of our wrongs.

- *Step Six*: Were entirely ready to have God remove all these defects of character.
- *Step Seven:* Humbly asked Him to remove our shortcomings.

This rigorous honesty is not about shame—it is about freedom. Naming our flaws in the presence of a compassionate witness can have a purifying effect. James Finley encourages seekers to find someone "who will neither invade us nor abandon us," someone who can embody God's mercy in human form.[7]

ILLUMINATION

IN THE ILLUMINATIVE STAGE, the soul begins to see with new eyes. Perception shifts, and so does behavior. Mystics describe this stage as the enlightening of our reason through faith. In AA circles, this is sometimes called "putting on a new pair of glasses." We become capable of imitating Christ—not perfectly, but with intention.

- *Step Eight*: Made a list of all persons we had harmed and became willing to make amends to them all.
- *Step Nine*: Made direct amends to such people wherever possible, except when to do so would injure them or others.
- *Step Ten*: Continued to take personal inventory and when we were wrong promptly admitted it.

With these steps, the spiritual journey is made incarnate. We become willing to take responsibility for the disconnection and resentment in our relationships. This does not mean we excuse or minimize the harmful behavior of others, but rather we "keep our side of the street clean." Making amends may not always lead to reconciliation, but it enacts an inward transformation: a shift from avoidance to engagement, from fear to humility.

Mystics have debated whether perfect union is possible in this life, but most agree that, through contemplation, we can taste it.

The book *Alcoholics Anonymous* states that "if we are painstaking about this phase of our development, we will be amazed before we are halfway through. We will intuitively know how to handle situations which used to baffle us."[8] This intuition is the fruit of removing the log from our own eyes (Matthew 7:5) so that we are able to see everything in a new light.

Step Ten invites us to make this way of life a daily practice. We ask God to illuminate the day that has just passed so that we can see where we have wandered off the path. Fr. Thomas Keating has said that this practice develops our ability to be "sensitive to responding to the needs of the present moment and also to the presence of God in every passing nanosecond of time."[9]

UNION

IF PURGATION IS descent and illumination is transformation, then union is the return—into intimacy with God and service to others. Mystics have debated whether perfect union is possible in this life, but most agree that, through contemplation, we can taste it.

- *Step Eleven*: Sought through prayer and meditation to improve our conscious contact with God as we understood Him, praying only for knowledge of His will for us and the power to carry that out.

- *Step Twelve*: Having had a spiritual awakening as the result of these steps, we tried to carry this message to alcoholics and to practice these principles in all our affairs.

Union is described here not as ecstasy, but as "conscious contact." It is daily, humble awareness of God's loving presence. For Teresa of Ávila (1515–1582), this awareness must bear fruit. The most certain sign that we love God "is that we have a genuine love for others."[10]

Union with God flows outward in service. The mystic becomes a "wounded healer"—one who, having changed course themselves, can now companion others. As the book *Alcoholics Anonymous* insists, "However far down the scale we have gone, we can see how our experience can benefit others."[11] The Twelve Steps embrace descent as the starting point of transformation, but rather than ascending to a superior plane of existence, we meet other sufferers where they are at. Our compassion for our own predicament and our powerlessness over it shines forth in true compassion and grace for others.

Read through the lens of Christian mysticism, the Twelve Steps reflect a living contemplative tradition—a rhythm of descent, transformation, and return. They offer a spiritual itinerary not just for addicts, but for all who seek healing, wholeness, and a life of service. Like the mystics before them, those who walk this path discover that union with God inevitably flows outward—in humility, compassion, and justice for the sake of the world.

Keep Your Heart Open in Hell

By Mirabai Starr

T HERE IS A LEGEND IN CHINESE BUDDHISM that depicts Quan Yin, the embodiment of compassion, traveling to the underworld to give solace to the dead. But the bodhisattva was not always a goddess. She was once a woman, named Miao Shan.

During the Tang Dynasty (618–907) in China, semi-independent kingdoms vied for power. Miao Shan's father, a king who wished to consolidate his influence, tried to marry off his daughter to a wealthy lord. Same old story of patriarchy and power. But Miao Shan refused, choosing instead the life of a Buddhist nun.

This was the last thing the king wanted, so he devised a plan to dissuade her. The king struck a backroom deal with the abbess of the local monastery to accept his daughter into her community and then pile on menial and unpleasant tasks, the kind of work reserved for enslaved people, so that Miao Shan would become disenchanted with religious life, come to her senses, and return home to be married.

But Miao Shan thrived in her labor. She loved working side by side with people she never would have encountered in her life of privilege: people with real lives, real troubles, and a vast capacity for enjoying the present moment. When her obligations mounted and she was not sure how she could tend to them all in the timeframe set for her by the abbess, the animals of the forest showed up to help her. Mice and rabbits, owls and spiders, all contributed their skills to get the job done. When she was ordered to clean the wounds of the dying and dispose of their bodily fluids, celestial spirits came to her aid, infusing her service with grace. Miao Shan accompanied the critically injured and the terminally ill, singing them through their deaths. And when they died, she followed them to the underworld, singing her songs to ease their way through the trials they encountered as they made their way into their next incarnations.

Miao Shan's intimacy with the dying brought her unmitigated joy. Which of course enraged her father. He ordered her execution. But as the executioner lifted his ax, Miao Shan gazed up at him with such compassion that he could not bear to kill her. Knowing he would be punished and probably killed himself, Miao Shan reassured the man that he would incur no karma from his action and urged him to go through with it. In anguish, he swung his ax. Just before landing on Miao Shan's neck, the blade shattered into a thousand pieces. Miao Shan was unharmed. Instead, a white tiger appeared and carried her away to a remote mountain, where she dedicated herself to Buddhist practices for the rest of her life, frequently visiting the underworld to provide comfort and care to those who were navigating between lives.

My friend Stephen Levine (1937–2016), one of the pioneers of the conscious-dying movement, was a big fan of Miao Shan. "Keep your heart open in hell," Stephen used to say. This was not a trite slogan or an inspirational meme. It was a spiritual instruction.

When we encounter suffering—on a personal or a global level—our conditioning may compel us to get away from it. We engineer our escape in all kinds of obvious and subtle ways. Blatant distractions might include the abuse of mind-altering substances, or overconsumption of material

It is tempting to repurpose some of the tools we have gathered to protect us against the realities of grief and loss.

possessions, or workaholism. More insidious methods could masquerade as spiritual beliefs and practices that we engage in the hope of transcending the pain. These latter tricks are known as "spiritual bypassing."

For those of us who have been on a path of awakening, it is tempting to repurpose some of the tools we have gathered to protect us against the realities of grief and loss. This is understandable. But it is not useful. It does not transform suffering; it simply compartmentalizes difficult experiences and we will eventually have to come to grips with them, by which time our "unattended sorrow" (as Stephen called it) may have become a driver in an ongoing sense of disconnection from our sacred source.

What might happen if, instead of trying to circumvent the flames of grief and loss or douse them with religious beliefs and prescribed prayers, we let ourselves down into the arms of fire? How about, instead of arming ourselves against suffering, we opt to keep our hearts open in hell?

This is the path of conscious grieving. It may feel counterintuitive at first, but it is one of the most transformational practices I know. When we feel assaulted by images of starvation in the Sudan, children bombed in Gaza, acres of unhoused folks on the streets of every city in the US, giant cracks in the polar icecaps and vast chunks breaking off and melting into eerily warm oceans, and species becoming extinct at lightning speed, who wouldn't want to change the channel, or turn over and go back to sleep? We would do anything sometimes to not feel our feelings. Yet, like Miao Shan, we can face the horror with bravery and embrace the broken with genuine joy. Our willingness to gather the suffering into our shattered hearts transforms the pain. Our own pain, and that of the world.

There is good reason why Quan Yin has been compared to Mother Mary. She stands rooted in the reality of anguish and loves us through our most unbearable experiences. We cry out, and she listens with her hundred ears, stands watch with her hundred eyes, reaches out with her hundred arms. She bestows an endless flow of mercy from the healing vessel she holds. There is nothing you could do to make her turn away from you. She will follow you into hell and sing you home.

We are all Quan Yin. The moment we choose to enter the center of our grief and keep our hearts open, we become bodhisattvas of compassion. When we bend to embrace the ravaged body of the human community, we are transfigured into a version of the Madonna. It is our birthright to step through the fiery gate of loss and into the sacred landscape of belonging. Contemplative practices teach us to not believe everything we think, and devotional practices water our hearts so that the seeds of compassion, concealed in the most harrowing spaces, may germinate and flourish. When we cultivate these inner gardens, we can nourish ourselves and feed the world.

I spend a lot of time sitting with bereaved beings. Mothers whose children have died of suicide or accidental overdoses, car crashes or cancer. Loving spouses whose partners have left them for someone else, sisters estranged from brothers, members of a congregation whose leadership has betrayed them. Elders who grieve the loss of their capacities, athletes whose injuries have permanently derailed their life's purpose. Immigrants fleeing unspeakable violence, only to encounter hatred and cruelty where they hoped to find refuge. In every case, I wish that these folks did not have to bear such sorrow. And yet each one seems to make their way to my door precisely because they have experienced the fires of loss and have detected the fragrance of the sacred emanating from those coals.

I have experienced this myself. The death of my teenaged daughter Jenny in a car accident in 2001 ripped the veils from my life and plunged me into numinous terrain. I am still making my way through this sacred space, and it continues to transform me.

Haven't you? Haven't you felt the presence of the divine, not *despite*, but rather *because of* your confrontation with an excruciating reality? To stay close to the metaphor of fire, grief is a forest fire that sweeps through our lives and burns the familiar landscape to the ground. It takes time for the smoke to clear so that we can breathe again and glimpse the sky, and much longer for new growth to emerge from soil replenished by the minerals released by the charred trees. The flames of grief can melt the protective layering around our hearts and grant us access to an intimate encounter with the divine.

The question is, what are we to do in the meantime? St. John of the Cross (1542–1591) would suggest: *nada*. Nothing. Rather, the invitation is to sit quietly amid the wreckage of our hearts and pay attention. Not as an act of spiritual strength-training, but as an offering of love. Love for your loved one who has died or left you, love for the body you have, love for the God who gave you life. Love for the world.

Try it right now. Take a moment to ponder one particular experience of loss. Allow yourself to recall the fresh flame of pain. Soften into the full range of feelings that arise. There may be agony, but there may also be something else, some radiance rising through the gloom, the contours of a majestic topography emerging as your eyes grow accustomed to the dark. Within the very heart of your broken heart, a presence you have longed for all your life is beckoning. Say a quiet yes. Accept the invitation. Allow yourself to be transmuted by your encounter with the fire of grief. You have nothing left to lose.

This is not a path for the spiritually complacent, for those who require easy answers to what happens when we die or conventional methods for mourning. It asks of us a kind of fierce courage to stay present in the heat of grief and let ourselves dissolve, releasing outmoded ideas of spiritual evolution and coming to peace with exactly what is. But it is not a penance, either. Grief as a transformational practice is much more about being than doing. It demands nothing and makes space for everything. It is an invitation to surrender to a love greater than the pain, a love that cannot help but seep through the torn seams of your broken heart, mending and rendering you a source of greater love in this broken world.

Engaged Contemplative Christianity as a Living, Life-Giving Tradition

By Brian McLaren

T HE FACT THAT YOU'RE READING *Oneing* tells me you feel some attraction to a community that integrates action and contemplation, with the emphasis on the *and*. For that reason, I'd like to invite you to reflect with me on what it means to be part of a tradition or lineage in general and of this tradition in particular.

BEING PART OF A TRADITION

TRADITIONS ARE CULTURAL communities that carry on, from generation to generation, ideas and practices (what I call *treasures*) in which they see great enduring value.

Like everything in this universe, traditions are constantly changing, even if the change occurs at a glacial pace. (Though these days we know that sometimes even glaciers change quickly.) Sometimes they change for the better. Sometimes they change for the worse.

Even if a tradition were to stay exactly the same, to be the same thing in a different environment is not the same thing. For example, to sit still on a chair in a meditation room for an hour without doing anything is one thing. It is a very different thing when you're sitting in your living room and you look out the window to see your neighbor's house in flames. Even if traditions resist change with all their strength, their changing environment changes who and what they are in the world.

These few insights about traditions help explain why we so often struggle with them. They have much to offer, but we have to decide how many of our 450,000 precious hours (a typical lifespan) we want to invest in a tradition, and which tradition or traditions are wisest to invest in.

Spiritual or engaged contemplative traditions intentionally seek to help us develop the inner life so that we can become better people and build better communities that contribute to a better world. If you invest some of your precious 450,000 hours in a healthy contemplative tradition, you might find the return on investment to be high, bringing great blessings to you as a participant. Those blessings can then flow out into the world around you. Let's call those kinds of spiritual traditions *life-giving*.

Other traditions might turn out to be a disappointment to you. They may even feel like a scam. Your investment of time brings you no substantial return, or whatever you gain is more than offset by the cost or harm you experience.

LIFE-GIVING OR DEATH-DEALING?

SOME TRADITIONS THAT helped people in the past may turn out to do harm in the present: The more you participate, the more they render you a less loving and more hateful human being, less forgiving and more vengeful, less generous and more selfish, less kind and more violent. Some of these *death-dealing traditions* continue to bring substantial benefit to insiders even as they inflict significant harm upon outsiders—even harming the Earth itself.

Traditions that were once death-dealing can change and become more benign or even beneficial over time. Conversely, traditions that are life-giving for millions of people in the present could be twisted into death-dealing traditions in the present or future.

We have no choice as to the tradition into which we were born. As we grow older, we must decide: Is this inherited tradition life-giving, death-dealing, or a mix of both? If it is in an unhealthy condition right now, is it improvable or salvageable? Does participating in it perpetuate harm? Is it time to migrate to a new spiritual tradition?

When we choose to invest our precious time in the most life-giving tradition we can find, we have a responsibility—we might call it a moral responsibility—to understand the tradition's core treasures: its deepest values, vision, practices, and insights; its origins, history, and leading figures. We also have a responsibility to face its shortcomings, missteps, imbalances, and current needs for growth, so we can someday, if possible, pass on an even better version of the tradition than we have received.

Many loyal members of a tradition do not understand this responsibility. They have been taught (explicitly or implicitly) that if they want to be truly faithful to the tradition, they must deny or minimize its past and present weaknesses and failures and lower their expectations to accept the status quo as sufficient. Their job, they are taught, is to perpetuate the version of the tradition that they received, without alteration, "forever and ever, amen," as if the tradition were perfect and in no need of adaptation or improvement.[1]

So, here we are. Every day, more and more of us find ourselves unable to perpetuate the religious traditions in which we were raised. We have

How will we help our tradition to grow, mature, and expand its influence for good?

experienced them as taking more than they give, or, in some cases, we fear they do more harm than good. We have made a great spiritual migration: We have left, often with tears, beloved inherited traditions we considered death-dealing and stubbornly resistant to change. If we hadn't found (or been found by) the tradition of engaged contemplative Christianity, many of us couldn't consider ourselves Christians anymore. We would find ourselves spiritually homeless.[2]

As we rejoice in this growing, life-giving, living tradition, we face important questions: How will we help our tradition to grow, mature, and expand its influence for good? How will we enrich and improve the tradition as it stands? How can we discern its present weaknesses, not in order to criticize and condemn the tradition, but in order to heal, strengthen, and energize it for greater fruitfulness in the future? What might the growing edges of our tradition be?

TEN GROWING EDGES

I WOULD LIKE TO suggest ten growing edges for our life-giving, living tradition. This list is certainly not complete. I will phrase each growing edge in terms of a question for you to consider and maybe even explore with others.

1. How can we understand and explain what we mean by *engaged contemplation* and the *engaged contemplative path* without using language that doesn't needlessly alienate potential participants, especially younger ones who will potentially carry on this tradition when we are gone? For example, many of us talk about the saints of our tradition as if everyone knows them, forgetting how few

people have any idea that they exist. We throw around technical terms like *nonduality*, *lectio divina*, *shadow*, or *theosis* because they have become precious to us, not realizing that for many, they are completely baffling. Without repeated explanation, our in-group jargon creates a wall rather than a bridge to meaning. How can we learn the language of the tradition and yet remember how to speak in plain English (or whatever language), in terms a normal person—even a child—can understand?[3]

2. How can we remember that "the sit" is one time-tested form of contemplative practice among many? How can we create ways to introduce diverse people of all ages to a variety of practice door-ways into this rich, diverse, living, life-giving tradition?

3. How can we keep clear the difference between maturing as contemplatives and becoming avid collectors of contemplative lore or proud achievers of contemplative status? It is so easy, as Catholic contemplative Thomas Merton (1915–1968) warned, to turn "being a contemplative" (or looking and sounding like one!) into a status that makes us feel superior, which then defeats the tradition's very goal of becoming more humble, just, loving, and connected human beings.

4. Speaking of language, here's a delicate but important question: How can we address the problems associated with precious words like *God* and *Jesus* and *Christianity*? Too many Christians wield these words like weapons. As a result, when many people hear *God*, they think of an angry judge waiting to send them to hell. Say *Jesus*, and they think of a white Jesus with an AR-15 spreading white supremacy, nationalism, and patriarchy. Identify with *Christianity*, and they think you are determined to keep women down, LGBTQ people afraid, and the Earth up for sale to the highest capitalist bidder. There are unintended consequences both to using these words without explanation and to avoiding them entirely. What can we do?[4]

5. More on words: How can we avoid using *engaged*, *contemplative*, and *Christian* in dualistic/binary/exclusive ways? We need to realize that some approaches to contemplation are less "engaged" with the world and its needs than others, and that's OK. Some forms of activism are less contemplative than others, and that's OK. And some forms of Christianity are more or less contemplative and

engaged, and that's OK. We are not *against* other traditions that have other approaches. Our task is to clearly define who and what this tradition is *for*, so we can be both clear and inviting to less-engaged contemplatives, to less-contemplative activists, and to a wide array of Christians and others for whom *contemplation, action,* and *Christian* are equally confusing concepts.[5]

6.   How can we plumb the depths of our tradition's ancient and medieval sources in ways that make sense in our contemporary world? For example, today's world is multicultural, and many of our sources are European. How can we broaden the tradition to include diverse voices from both past and present without neglecting the tradition's older European resources?[6] How can we achieve a vital both/and?

7.   How can we keep our life-giving tradition a *living* tradition by keeping it a *learning* tradition? How can we be in truly respectful conversation with contemplatives of other faith traditions, sharing our unique treasures, so we can learn from and with one another? How can we be in meaningful conversation with contemplative and active thinkers in the sciences and other academic fields: neuroscience, evolutionary biology, economics, social and personal psychology, history, political science, ecology? For *engaged* contemplatives, these conversations are urgently important in light of the poly-crisis we face—climate change and ecological overshoot, economic injustice and inequality, political decay and division, the proliferation of weapons, artificial intelligence, and more. How, in times of emergency and unraveling, can we collaborate broadly in the "great turning" upon which our future depends?

8.   How can each of us who have a direct connection to and affection for a beloved living leader cherish the founder's vision, example, and body of work—without turning their legacy into a museum? How can we love and honor our great leaders by continuing their work, or, as Jim Finley has said of Richard Rohr, how can we be about what our beloved leaders have been about, instead of simply being about our leaders?[7]

9.   How can engaged contemplatives express our spirituality in action in a time when old systems and structures are crumbling? Many of us were trained in the activism of the 1960s or 2010s, when political, social, and religious systems were still somewhat intact and

democratic governments still had some sway over the hyper-wealthy. But the world has changed and is changing. What will the new activism look like if current trends toward authoritarianism and oligarchy continue? What if we face a long period of time when conditions get worse before they get better? What if conditions will someday get better, but in a new way that we cannot now even imagine? How can contemplative activism contribute to the emergence of a new activism for a new time? How can we, through contemplation and action, discern the seeds that must be planted for a future not our own? How can contemplative wisdom be disseminated to help people deal with the stresses and fears of a world in turmoil?

10. How can alliances be built with existing institutions to both preserve and spread the life-giving treasures of our tradition? For example, can we collaborate with congregations, seminaries, denominations, mission agencies, schools and colleges, online entities, and other organizations to further our shared work of supporting personal transformation that leads to loving, transformative action in our troubled world? Can we bring the resources of contemplation and action to bear on liturgy, so liturgy becomes a transformative contemplative experience for millions of people—as it was intended to be? Can we train clergy and educators to bring the gifts of this tradition to their congregants and classrooms? If not, what will that mean? If so, where do we begin?

Of course, this list is incomplete. What questions would you add to the list, because you no doubt see things that I don't?

As I stated at the beginning, to be part of a life-giving tradition brings with it a moral responsibility to make it even better as we pass it on to future generations.

Seven Themes of an Alternative Orthodoxy

By Richard Rohr

THE PHRASE "ALTERNATIVE ORTHODOXY" is not something I remember hearing in my formal studies. We used to speak of it in the seminary as the Franciscan Opinion. My Franciscan professors would invariably teach the mainline opinion, and then they'd say, "Of course, we have our own opinion." It wasn't said in a contentious way, but it made us aware, on point after point, that we as Franciscans are not really in total compliance, if that's the right word, with mainline Roman Catholicism, even though we were clearly not in opposition to it either. How we pulled that off still amazes me!

As the years went on at the Center for Action and Contemplation (CAC), I realized that's what we were doing too. For some, the very term Alternative Orthodoxy might seem like a contradiction: "Well, if it's alternative, then it's not orthodox Christianity." Yet, that's exactly the point we want to make: You can emphasize different things and still be orthodox.[1]

Eventually, we identified what we've called Seven Themes of an Alternative Orthodoxy that summarize what I have taught over the years. A previous CAC executive director came to me one day and said, "Richard, you talk about so many things, but what really are your underlying, recurring major themes?" I took two or three months to look at my teachings and try to identify the foundational elements, then shared them with her. She looked at the seven themes and said, "We have the curriculum for a school." These themes shaped our Living School.

THEME ONE:

Scripture as validated by experience, and experience as validated by Tradition, are good scales for one's spiritual worldview.

THE FIRST THEME in our Living School became our methodology. I call this our "tricycle" that moves us forward. If you don't declare your methodology as a teacher, you can basically stand up and say anything. I'm afraid that's what a lot of preachers and teachers do. People have every right to ask, "By what authority do you say that?" So, I declare my authority at the beginning, saying that it's three-wheeled like a tricycle.

The front wheel is something that Orthodox, Catholic, and Protestant Christians were not taught much about: experience. I make this the front wheel because we filter Scripture and Tradition through our own experience. We cannot not do this. It's common sense. It's obvious, but we often have not had the courage to state the obvious.

Scripture is validated by the two other wheels of our tricycle: experience and Tradition. If it's true—and this is an act of faith—then it must somehow be found in Scripture, or at least not directly contradicted by it. We look for validation in Tradition through writings from mystics, saints, prophets, councils of the church, and fathers and mothers of the church. We Catholics pretended, not dishonestly, that all our teaching was based on Tradition with a big "T," but it was really Italian tradition, French tradition, German tradition—with a little "t."

We have made it our work to try to get back to the big "T." What are the truths that keep reoccurring? What keeps coming back, century after century? What do wise people keep saying? If it's from the Holy Spirit, it will keep being discovered, again and again. The Catholic intellectual Thomas Aquinas (1225–1274) held that if it's true, it is from the Holy Spirit.[2]

While experience is the front wheel of the tricycle, it is constantly balanced and critiqued by Scripture and Tradition. When all three work together in someone, we have a very wise person. That's the easiest way to say it. At the CAC, we're interested in raising up wise people, not argumentative or righteous people.

THEME TWO:

If God is Trinity and Jesus is the face of God, then it is a benevolent universe. God is not someone to be afraid of, but is the Ground of Being and on our side.

WE NEED TO be begin with a clear understanding of God. Who do we say God is? Is God a tyrant, dictator, or judge? Most Christians were not taught this very well. The Christian tradition introduced the Trinity, which is a word not found in Scripture. God is not one. God is a communion, a relationship of eternal, infinite, flowing of love between three. The placeholder names that we gave to these three were "Father," "Son," and "Holy Spirit."

We don't know how to picture a divine flow of infinite love, so we look at Jesus, who is the living image of God that humanity can look at. When we do, it is a benevolent universe. In other words, religion is not a scary thing. I've been a priest for over fifty years and have preached in forty-five countries, and I've seen that the vast majority of Christians are not in love with God. They're afraid of God. We have a lot of work to do to transform that image of God as someone to be afraid of and to say it is a benevolent universe.

We can't imagine infinite love, so we pulled God down to the tit-for-tat level on which we operate, measuring "this much" sin or "that much" punishment. Danté's *Divine Comedy* is a great piece of literature, but it's horrible theology. It's about rewarding or punishing people who have "this much" goodness with "this much" reward.

But God isn't into reward and punishment. God isn't into win-lose. The very nature of God is to work for win/win. God wins, and we win too. When we can transfer our psyche to a win-win universe that doesn't need reward and punishment, we've created the foundation for a true and healing Christianity.

What we have taught in the Living School and at the CAC is that the shape of God is the shape of the human soul and the shape of everything else. As Genesis 1 puts it, we were created in the "image" and "likeness" of God. If God is infinite love, then—believe it or not—each soul is a source of implanted love. God is not someone to be afraid of but is the very ground of our being.

THEME THREE:

For those who see deeply, there is only one reality. By reason of the incarnation, there is no truthful distinction between sacred and profane.

GOD IS THREE, but God is also one. Out of diversity, when love is added, we have unity. The sciences are helping us to understand this, from molecular biology to neuroscience, planetary science, and astrophysics. They're all recognizing that everything exists in relationship to everything else. Nothing is solitary in the universe. Everything is connected.

Let me put this in a theological frame. The only thing that separates us from God is the thought that we're separate from God. A tree doesn't think the way we think. It simply does its tree thing, knowing it's connected. Science understands now about how trees talk to one another and how all trees are connected to one another. They warn one another when there's poison in the ground. It seems that cells, molecules, and animals do their thing more than we do our thing!

When we see deeply, we will also see with love.

All reality is sacred, but religion usually begins by declaring things sinful, profane, or dirty. Religion is always declaring what's bad instead of recognizing what's holy about everything. We don't have enough time on this planet to decide who's worthy and who's unworthy. It's not our job to decide. It's none of our business, because it's all holy, and it was all created with a divine DNA.

There is one God who created all things: dogs, trees, and us. Everything carries and holds the divine fingerprint. This is the good news that Jesus came to give us, but we turned it into bad news so we could have a reason to hate other races, religions, and nations. Christian nations are historically no better than anybody else. The history of Europe is a history of war, with good French Catholics hating good English Catholics. But God doesn't hate anyone. There's only one reality for those who see deeply. The work of the CAC is the teaching of contemplation, which is to teach how to see deeply. When we see deeply, we will also see with love.

THEME FOUR:

Everything belongs. No one needs to be punished, scapegoated, or excluded. We cannot directly fight or separate ourselves from evil or untruth. Darkness becomes apparent when exposed to the light.

MOST OF US were not taught that everything belongs. We have spent most of history deciding who doesn't belong and then thinking we have every right to kill, exclude, or punish them. There isn't a single culture that doesn't hate another country, another nation, another race, another gender, another class. What we call history is filled with class wars, nation-state wars, and culture wars. Once we choose our side, we believe, for some reason, that we are given permission to hate the other side. That's called the scapegoat mechanism. René Girard (1923–2015), the French anthropologist, said that scapegoating is found in every single culture of the world, and it's almost entirely unconscious. We don't realize that's what we're doing. As Jesus said from the cross, "Father, forgive them. They don't know what they're doing" (Luke 23:34). We really don't. No one needs to be punished or scapegoated.

We cannot directly fight or separate ourselves from evil because it's everywhere. The only way evil succeeds is by disguising itself as good. I can get away with stating this as a priest: The best hiding place for evil is religion. All we have to do is put God's name to it, and we can justify slavery, apartheid, torture, and the Spanish Inquisition. The safest way to feel no guilt about our hatred or meanspiritedness is to find a scripture that justifies it, so we think we are doing it for God. Jesus said, "A time is coming when those who kill you will think they are doing a holy service to God" (John 16:2).

The American form of Christianity legitimated slaveholding from the very beginning. Any form of Christianity that can legitimate making the body of Christ into people you can whip, rape, punish, and torture is so far from anything Jesus talked about that it's not worthy of being called Christianity.

We are all involved in evil systems. General and President Dwight Eisenhower (1890–1969) was from my home state of Kansas. After he left office as president, he predicted that the United States would become totally controlled by the military-industrial complex. The apostle Paul called such a system, in his premodern language, "thrones, dominions, principalities, and powers" (Colossians 1:16). These are the institutions that are larger than life.

Don't you feel sorry for God, that the infinite flow of love has to put up with all this? We're still in the early centuries of evolution. Christianity is still a childish religion.

THEME FIVE:

The "separate self" is the major problem, not the shadow self which only takes deeper forms of disguise.

THE SHADOW IS not evil. It's just what we don't want to see about ourselves. It is what we're not ready to see about ourselves or our country, religion, class, gender, or group. Every human being I've met has had a rather well-disguised shadow which they didn't want other people to know about. Their spouse sees it, and anybody who gets close to them sees it. But people who know them in a casual way don't get to see it. We all put our *bella figura*, our good face, forward so everybody will like us.

This is understandable and probably necessary for survival in what I call the first half of life. But by the second half of life, it starts becoming toxic. Everybody else knows you're an angry old man except you! Everybody else knows you're a prejudiced racist except you. That's how well the shadow self disguises itself.

The Swiss psychologist Carl Jung (1875–1961) popularized the concept and wisely chose the word *shadow*. The shadow is not light or darkness. It's a mixture of the two. The secret is to recognize that the self that you're so ashamed and afraid of actually has some light in it. The shadow has much to teach you about yourself, about reality, and mostly about love. Once you can learn to forgive your own shadow and be honest about your shadow, you start becoming a very compassionate human being, because everybody else is fighting the same battle. We're all wounded in ways we don't want anybody else to see.

The goal of spirituality—and, I must say, the goal of religion—is to unite the self, in all its shadowy-ness and woundedness, to God. It's the mystery of forgiveness: We will "know salvation by the forgiveness of sin" (Luke 1:77). Unless we've been forgiven for some really stupid things that we've done— and we've all done some really stupid things—we'll never know what God's infinite love feels like. So shadow isn't bad. Shadow is just dangerous when it's denied. Once we've faced our shadow, we're home free.

The goal of spirituality is union with God, not perfection within ourself. We don't have to be perfect. We just have to live in union. It's not about being correct. It's about being connected. It is an entirely different agenda to remain connected at every level: the human level; the divine level; the animal level; the plant, tree, grass, and flower level. Once we start uniting with reality, which is contemplation, it never stops. There's always another thing to commune with, to connect with, to forgive. Soon, it becomes a way of life. Our simple word for that is *love*. We can't start loving reality unless we forgive the shadow part of everything.

THEME SIX:

The path of descent is the path of transformation. Darkness, failure, relapse, death, and woundedness are our primary teachers, rather than ideas or doctrines.

MUCH OF CHRISTIANITY and most of the world's religions have been paths of ascent. We are always trying to climb up higher, to be purer, holier, and more correct. We want to rid ourselves of all impurities so we can be worthy of God—and we can never succeed at that path of ascent. The rules will always get stricter and stricter. It's why there are a lot of angry, old Christians who are very judgmental of anybody who isn't as perfect as they are.

The path of *descent* is the path of transformation. In other words, darkness, failure, relapse, woundedness, and many forms of death are our primary teachers. Ideas and doctrines really don't teach us anything. What teaches us in an unforgettable way is when we hit bottom: when we fall apart, when we lose a job, when our marriage fails, when our child dies. We're never the same after such things, if we allow them to teach us.

Christianity has a very strange logo: a naked, bleeding man dying on a cross. That's our brand, our marker. Did you ever think about how ridiculous that is? If one of us was going to found a religion and come up with a logo, it wouldn't be a picture of abject failure. But one group that's discovered this are the people in Alcoholics Anonymous: people in recovery working the Twelve Steps.

Step 1 is: "We admitted we were powerless over alcohol—that our lives had become unmanageable." We usually have to hit bottom before we start seeking out where the top really is. When all is said and done, we come to God by doing it wrong more than by doing it right. It's the place within us where we know we're not that perfect, or that loving, or that forgiving, or that simple and humble, like Jesus. When we can accept and allow that truth about ourselves and live in that kind of humility, we'll be happy old men and women. We won't have anything to prove, anything to protect, anything to deny, or any *bella figura* to promote. I am who I am, who I am, who I am.

That's the path of descent. Once you've done that journey, you're ready to enter eternal communion, because you've allowed God to love you in your nothingness.

THEME SEVEN:

Nonduality is the highest level of consciousness. Divine union, not private perfection, is the goal of all religion.

NON-DUALITY IS a word that has been used more by people in the East, in Hinduism, Taoism, and Buddhism. Things are not totally one, but they're not two either. The term we Catholics used was "unitive thinking," to see things in their unity. Nondual thinking allows us to think in a paradoxical way and to live with what seem like contraries. What seems contrary is really just coming at things at a different level and from a different side.

I will go so far as to say that most of reality is paradoxical. It's filled with things that look like contradictions, but upon closer examination, they are not. The 150-year-old cottonwood tree at our Center is alive, but although we trim it every few years, it's already dying. It will die completely in short order, probably within the next twenty years, although some live to 200. It's living, and it's dying—at the same time. Christians understand this in the mystery that we call Jesus Christ: Christ has died, Christ is risen, Christ will come again.

Everything is living, everything is dying. Everything is recurring. It never stops. The ultimate paradox is that life and death are not contraries. Life and death do not cancel one another out. Death is not the opposite of life, and life is not the opposite of death. They include one another. Darkness includes light, and light includes darkness.

So, to be able to live nondually, with paradox, ambiguity, and imperfection, is the highest level of consciousness. What seems like imperfection is the highest level of consciousness! That's what allows us to be forgiving people. Reality doesn't need to be perfect before we love it. Divine union, not private perfection, is the goal of all religion. Once we can think in a unitive way, where we can put opposites together, we can solve most moral dilemmas. We can forgive people. We can recognize that our simple binaries are never true. The best ally of God is reality, what is, not what we want it to be.

Every moral issue has that kind of ambiguity to it. Unless you have a tolerance for ambiguity and a sympathy for paradox, you'll never be a loving or happy person.

But if you can back up your statements with, "The contrary is also true," you will be a much happier person. You won't feel you need to change, fix, control, or even understand everything. That's contemplation—when you don't need to understand. Whoever gave you the right to understand everything?

These Seven Themes give us some common terrain, a common view of human and divine nature, and how they are made to work together. That's what religion should be teaching us. And the goal, at the end of life, is that we finally know it's all about love.[3]

Modern Mystics in the Movements:

Incarnating Holy Resistance, Radical Hope, and Contemplative Activism

By Alison McCrary

"**H**OPE IS BEING able to see that there is light despite all of the darkness," Archbishop Desmond Tutu (1931–2021) said.[1] There's no shortage of "darkness" in our world. Climate catastrophe looms. Systems are collapsing. Oligarchy rules. Authoritarianism and war are on the rise. Power is exchanged for loyalty. The project of capitalism has turned into medieval feudalism, where politics and economics are the same in terms of who has power. Colonial projects and genocides expand at the hands of those with wealth. White supremacy gains power and more protections. Funding cuts continue to grow economic disparities between the poor and the one percent. And the list goes on.

Yet, in the midst of such suffering and injustice, hope is a fundamental practice in our Christian tradition. Such hope isn't just wishful thinking or optimism, but rather the ability to recognize, find, and cultivate beauty, light, and life, even when surrounded by gloom, darkness, and death. A core tenet of our theology and belief, the Paschal Mystery of life, suffering, death, and resurrection, invites us to believe and live into a hope that death will never have the final word. Only love will. We are called to live a life of hope and love as we cultivate social justice and social healing in the world.

But how do we strategize, organize, and advocate to create systemic change without living in a state of despair, hopelessness, defeat, or anger? This article explores ten practices I've identified for contemplative activists in social justice movements. These invitations ground us for the long haul as we live out our gospel mandate of social justice. They help us hold and work to transform the pain of the world while being fed internally by our personal practices and reflection.

I'll also share how we can cultivate a foundational practice of an inner sensing of the divine, combined with action for liberation through intention, attention, and repetition. Thomas Merton's insight that "Contemplation gives birth to social action by teaching the contemplation that she and others are one"[2] reinforces that contemplation and action are not separate, but are interwoven threads of a single, transformative life.

When we engage in actions of justice, healing, hope, and holy resistance to oppression, we are offering and creating sacraments. A sacrament is defined as a public action or ritual that can be seen, a visible sign imparting an invisible grace from God, and a means or symbol of a spiritual reality. Sacraments are where God is present. Sacraments require a physical component, an incarnation, an act, or an action. Traditionally, in the Catholic faith, these are the rites of Baptism, Confirmation, Eucharist, Reconciliation (Confession), Anointing of the Sick, Matrimony, and Holy Orders.

Yet our relationship with God deepens the more places we experience God. Encounters with the divine occur through others in unexpected ways. From protests to political engagement acts such as voting, these can be and are visible symbols of the reality of God in the world and a channel for God's grace to manifest.

Acts of sacramental value transform our consciousness to evolve new realities aligned with divine mystery and love. They move us toward creating a world where all can be "done on earth as it is in heaven." Those whom I've accompanied and worked alongside as a social-justice-movement lawyer, community organizer, restorative-justice practitioner, and Spiritual Advisor on death row for the past two decades have helped me grow in this ability.

Among issues of immigrants' rights, environmental justice, gender jus-tice, a free Palestine, housing rights, land justice, healthcare rights, racial justice, civil rights, queer liberation, healing justice, community care, voting rights, cultural rights, Indigenous liberation, and other issues, one group of people I have been asked to "stand" with are those facing executions as they sit on death row. They request that I serve as their Spiritual Advisor, a volunteer position approved by the prison to provide spiritual accompani-ment and emotional support to them until their death. The Spiritual Advisor is the only one allowed in the death chamber during an execution. In this work, I'm reminded of the lyrics in Ben E. King's 1961 song, "Stand By Me":

> When the night has come
> And the land is dark
> And the moon is the only light we'll see,
> No I won't be afraid
> Oh, I won't be afraid
> Just as long as you stand, stand by me.[3]

Executions are always shrouded in secrecy. Standing by those facing state-sanctioned executions, we try to not be afraid. We know that we are never alone. We walk with each other until a natural death or until our government takes the life of those on the row "when the night has come" and "the land is dark."

As we work for this future as people on a spiritual journey... we are called to cultivate a contemplative life.

Where are we called to stand? Who are we called to stand with? What do we need to learn or experience to know where we stand? Where are we fearful of standing?

I met Jessie Hoffman twenty years ago on death row at Angola State Penitentiary in Louisiana, the largest prison in the United States. When he was 18 years old, Jessie was found guilty of the rape and murder of Molly Elliott. Growing up in extreme poverty with multi-generational trauma and abuse, his own life was one of terror and neglect by the failed systems designed to protect children. After 27 years on death row, like all of us who grow and evolve over time, healing from our own wounds and learning to live differently than the world may have taught us to be, Jessie became a transformed person, a practicing and devout Buddhist. He moved with a mystical nature and lived a life of reflection and depth. His demeanor and positive attitude seemed more challenging for those of us to cultivate in society than for one to cultivate in a solitary-confinement prison cell.

Jessie was killed in our name by the government on March 18, 2025, but he wanted us to remember and to live into hope. Before his state-sanctioned execution by suffocation by gas, he asked that his memorial service be a celebration of life and of what is good. As he calmly walked to the execution chamber, he wore a t-shirt that read "Life's Row." Some men on death row prefer to call it "life's row," even up to the moment of their death.

My conversations with Jessie led me to believe that Jessie didn't seem to fear death by execution like most of us would. "Do not be afraid" and "have no fear" appear in our Christian scriptures 365 times. Christian tradition teaches us to live in the light rather than the darkness and live in hope rather than fear. I have seen Jessie Hoffman and those most on the margins of society live that out and serve as a model for the rest of us.

Jessie's impending death activated more people to work for ending the death penalty than at any other time in the history of Louisiana. Hundreds of faith leaders sent letters to our Governor. Dozens of business owners came together. Veterinarians organized, wrote letters, and held press conferences, sharing how their professional code of ethics does not allow them to gas dogs and cats. Jews made statements against the method of gassing, as it reminded them of what was used on their ancestors during the Holocaust. People woke up. Hope is a powerful force in helping individuals and communities wake up and take action in the face of injustice and violence.

Historian and philosopher Howard Zinn wrote:

> To be hopeful in bad times is not just foolishly romantic. It is based on the fact that human history is a history not only of cruelty, but also of compassion, sacrifice, courage, kindness. What we choose to emphasize in this complex history will determine our lives. If we see only the worst, it destroys our capacity to do something. If we remember those times and places—and there are so many— where people have behaved magnificently, this gives us the energy to act, and at least the possibility of sending this spinning top of a world in a different direction. And if we do act, in however small a way, we don't have to wait for some grand utopian future. The future is an infinite succession of presents, and to live now as we think human beings should live, in defiance of all that is bad around us, is itself a marvelous victory.[4]

As we work for this future as people on a spiritual journey, engaging in action for liberation in accordance with our Christian tradition, we are called to cultivate a contemplative life. "Contemplative activism" can be embodied through these ten practices:

1. Ground ourselves in spiritual practices. Know our practices. Cultivate an inner life.

2. Decolonize our lives and the systems that perpetuate colonized behaviors and mentalities.

3. Listen deeply to others, especially those on the margins of the margins.

4. Have a willingness to challenge power and build collective power.

5. Follow the leadership of those closest to the pain or the problem.

6. Build genuine relationships with those you are working with and advocating for.

7. Cultivate community and care.

8. Maintain an ever-evolving and deepening political analysis, values, and language.

9. Take risks.

10. Hold onto radical hope.

Each of the above practices also calls us to cultivate a practice of presence: to the divine, within our bodies, with our feelings (grief, joy, despair, hope), to and with another person, in the face of a person or institution causing harm, with nature, and to what is wanting to be revealed and created.

One of my teachers was Fr. Dan Berrigan (1921–2016), a Jesuit priest, pacifist, and draft-card burner during the United States War in Vietnam. A story told about Fr. Berrigan is that when asked to give a high school commencement speech, he walked up to the podium and is attributed as saying, "Know where you stand and stand there" and then sat down.

Who has asked you to stand by them in times of oppression, suffering, pain, and death? Who did you choose to stand by in their darkest moment? What support do you need to stand where you feel called to stand?

Being present, living into the ten practices of a contemplative activist, and staying grounded in our contemplative practices can awaken us to a new awareness of the divine dwelling within and among us as we work for good and move Martin Luther King Jr.'s "arc of justice" toward liberation.

As we do so, our own being and the divine being become more and more mysteriously interwoven. Contemplative activism is for everyone, not just a select few. We are called to reflect on the suffering of the world, our role in it, and what we are called to do in light of it. Contemplation invites us into the direct experience of God, and we can respond and act from a grounded and rooted space.

To cultivate a regular practice of an inner sensing of the divine, combined with action for liberation, three aspects are required: Intention, Attention, and Repetition.

1. *Intention*: We set the intention to be open to the divine energy within us. This means aligning ourselves with divine mystery and divine love.

2. *Attention*: What we give our attention to reflects our values. Attention also shifts our consciousness and makes way for meaningful reflection.

3. *Repetition*: Prayer is a repetitive activity that cultivates and sends positive energy out into the world. It may occur in the solitude and silence of our home prayer space, or it may be praying with our feet on the streets in protest to an injustice. Prayer is our way of being in relationship with the divine. Energy fields are forever changed when we cultivate and send out prayerful energy. We repeat prayer over and over again in the ways we learn and are learning to deepen and grow in this relationship to create the world we want to see.

What we give our intention, attention, and repetition to creates a foundational practice for action, grounded in our Christian contemplative tradition. Our world and our movements need us to create ways to confront and change systems in creative ways. We need to learn from others in global movements of social change and build infrastructure for shared collaboration, learning, support, and collective work.

The inner transformations needed to do this for the long haul create a reserve in our soul for when we experience despair, hopelessness, resentment, guilt, shame, or depletion. This reserve also helps us to hold onto a radical hope that lives in the marrow of our bones, allowing us to ignite loving action in the world.

May we weave a tapestry of contemplative practices that ground us in an ever-deepening ability to live in holy resistance, radical hope, and a life of contemplative activism. May we each become a dynamic force for liberation and love and answer the call to become a modern mystic in our social movements today. This is our birthright.

Let This Silence Become a Bridge

By Drew Jackson

I wake in the morning and sink down into the quiet Center.

Before the news and the heartbreak.

Before the world becomes all fire and brimstone.

Tell me, is this salvation?

I could stay here, alone and away.

I could place my life in the company of the undisturbed.

But if I do, I will surely lose You.

Friend of Sorrows. Acquaintance of Grief.

Let this silence, then, become a bridge.

Let me walk it to where Love is.

At the edges. Amidst the rubble.

Trudging among the bones

Where the prophets call to the four winds

And a Voice cries out saying *Live! Live!*

Let this silence become a forgotten thing

If it does not lead me to the hill

Outside the camp.[1]

Recommended Reading

The Silent God and the Silenced:
Mysticism and Contemplation Amid Suffering

Min-Ah Cho
Georgetown University Press, 2025

A Book Review by Lee Staman

MIN-AH CHO'S *The Silent God and the Silenced* is a timely theological exploration that delves into the paradoxes of silence—both divine and human—in the context of suffering, mysticism, and contemplation. I found this description by Cho helpful: "Mysticism is a dimension of experience and contemplation a dimension of disposition, both of which inevitably surpass human language and therefore find the best expression in silence."[1]

At the heart of Cho's project lies a radical redefinition of silence. Rather than viewing it simply as the absence of speech or divine response, Cho insists that silence can be an active form of communication and even revelation. She challenges inherited dichotomies—speech versus silence, action versus passivity—arguing that silence itself signals presence, protest, and creative possibility.

This reimagining is rooted in Christian mysticism: Evagrius Ponticus's apophatic theology (which privileges an unknowable God beyond all positive description), Hadewijch of Antwerp's ecstatic poetry, and Simone

Weil's insistence on attention as a spiritual practice. Cho situates these sources alongside Theresa Hak Kyung Cha, whose narratives speak to linguistic displacement, and Arundhati Roy, whose writings expose structural violence, to demonstrate how silence can function as resistance within oppressive contexts.

Throughout, Cho emphasizes that silence is not an escapist retreat but a deeply engaged stance: a way to unmask dominant narratives, amplify unheard voices, and attend to the suffering of others. She posits that, in an age of relentless noise—social-media clamor, political posturing, and constant information—true attentiveness requires an embrace of silence both internally (as contemplative discipline) and externally (as solidarity with those whose stories have been suppressed).

Cho organizes her argument across five chapters, each building upon the last to deepen the reader's grasp of silence in its various dimensions. She begins by suggesting that everyday silences already carry within them both divine presence and human absence, inviting a posture of listening that extends beyond words. Drawing from Max Picard's work, *The World of Silence*, she stresses that "silence is not something lacking but something that surpasses the dichotomy between things and no-things. Silence precedes and embraces all beings we find in the world and ultimately prepares us for union with the divine."[2]

This foundational chapter sets the stage for a theological inquiry into how silence manifests in both mundane and sacred realms. Moving into biblical territory, Cho traces how silence emerges as a space of divine action, turning to the paradoxical silence of the resurrection. Rather than depicting the empty tomb as a simple triumphant declaration, Cho reads its silence as an invitation to attend to the quiet cries of those awaiting renewal. Engaging Simone Weil's notion of attention, she suggests that the tomb's quiet beckons believers into vulnerability, listening for divine presence amid absence and mourning. This section blends reflections on ancient mysticism with contemporary ethical imperatives—prompting readers to notice unuttered pain: refugees buried at sea, victims of systemic racism, survivors of gender-based violence. The empty tomb's silence thus becomes a summons to solidarity rather than abstraction. The gospel women who visit the tomb at dawn bear witness not just by speaking but by their very presence in the liminal hours. Cho pairs these scriptural silences with Theresa Hak Kyung Cha's experimental texts on diaspora and violence, drawing parallels between gospel quiet and modern experiences of exile.

Toward the end, Cho explores how silence can paradoxically signify joy. This silent joy, she argues, calls believers to be laid bare before God, ready to be shaped by the Spirit's quiet work. In a world that prizes noise, this void (drawing from Simone Weil) becomes a radical space of resistance—a refusal to commodify suffering and an invitation to create solidarity across differences. At one point, she notes that "the silent God and the silenced unite in the empty tomb and the voids of the world, which become our place to come and stay, with all our brokenness and ineffable wounds."[3]

Cho brings the book to a close by proposing silence as an inherently relational phenomenon. Cho envisions concentric circles: One's inward movement into contemplative quiet must extend outward into communal listening for those who remain unheard. This concentric dynamic—interior silence rippling into activist solidarity—offers a spiritual discipline attuned to both God's silent presence and the world's suffering.

Overall, Cho's analysis of silence as a form of resistance stands out as one of the most original contributions. In a culture saturated with noise, silence becomes a refusal to participate. It is a way to reclaim agency and bear witness to suffering without exploiting it. Cho concisely states, "In waiting we listen to God, who listens to the silenced core of ourselves and others."[4] Through her readings of contemporary artists and writers, Cho shows how silence disrupts dominating narratives and opens new avenues for meaning. Silence, in her hands, is not passive but radically subversive.[5]

Contributors

RACHEL WHEELER is the author of three books, the most recent being *Radical Kinship: A Christian Ecospirituality*. She teaches at the University of Portland and is an oblate of Saint John's Abbey in Collegeville, Minnesota. Her current work engages ecoanxiety, collapse studies, and the Christian desert tradition.

ADAM BUCKO is an Episcopal priest and teacher of contemplative spirituality. He is the author most recently of *Let Your Heartbreak Be Your Guide: Lessons in Engaged Contemplation*. He serves as the Director of the Center for Spiritual Imagination and is a vowed member of the new monastic Community of the Incarnation.

KATIE GORDON is a spiritual seeker grounded in Benedictine tradition. She is the Coordinator of Monasteries of the Heart, an online movement that translates monastic wisdom for contemporary seekers, and writes a Substack called Following the Monastic Impulse that shares insights on the evolution and expansion of the monastic call today.

E. TREY CLARK is assistant professor of preaching and spiritual formation at Fuller Theological Seminary. He is the author of *Black Contemplative Preaching: A Hidden History of Prayer, Proclamation, and Prophetic Witness*. He lives with his family in Southern California.

THE REV. CASSIDY HALL (she/her), MA, MDiv, MTS, is the author of *Queering Contemplation: Finding Queerness in the Roots and Future of Contemplative Spirituality.* She is an award-winning filmmaker, podcaster, and ordained in the United Church of Christ. Her podcasts include *Encountering Silence, Contemplating Now,* and *Queering Contemplation.* Her films include *In Pursuit of Silence* and *Day of a Stranger.* Visit https://cassidyhall.com/.

THE REV. DR. BARBARA A. HOLMES (1943–2024) was a spiritual teacher and writer focused on African American spirituality, mysticism, cosmology, and culture. She was President Emerita of United Theological Seminary of the Twin Cities and also served as Vice President of Academic Affairs and Dean of Memphis Theological Seminary.

RICHARD ROHR is founder of the CAC and a globally recognized Franciscan friar and ecumenical teacher whose work bears witness to the deep wisdom of Christian mysticism. His many books include *The Universal Christ, Falling Upward,* and *Breathing Under Water.* His work has been featured on Oprah's *Super Soul Sunday,* Krista Tippett's *On Being,* and in *The New Yorker* and *Harper's Magazine.*

DR. CARMEN ACEVEDO BUTCHER is an award-winning translator and teacher, poet, contemplative workshop leader, and CAC Affiliate Faculty member. She holds a doctorate in Medieval Studies from the University of Georgia and teaches at the University of California, Berkeley. She has translated Brother Lawrence's *Practice of the Presence, Cloud of Unknowing,* Hildegard of Bingen, and others. Visit https://www.carmenbutcher.com/.

DOUGLAS E. CHRISTIE, PhD is Professor Emeritus of Theological Studies at Bellarmine College of Liberal Arts, Loyola Marymount University. He is the founding editor of *Spiritus: A Journal of Christian Spirituality* and author of *The Insurmountable Darkness of Love: Loss, Contemplative Practice and the Common Life.* Visit https://bellarmine.lmu.edu/theologicalstudies/faculty/?expert=douglas.christie.

ELISE LOEHNEN is the author of the *New York Times* bestseller, *On Our Best Behavior*, as well as the upcoming workbook companion, *Choosing Wholeness Over Goodness*. She's the host of the podcast *Pulling the Thread*. She lives in Los Angeles with her husband and two sons.

CHRISTINE VALTERS PAINTNER, PhD, REACE, OblSB is the online Abbess of Abbey of the Arts, a virtual monastery and global community of dancing monks and mystics seeking to integrate contemplative practice and creative expression. She is author of over twenty books on spirituality and lives in Ireland with her husband John.

KRISTIN VIEIRA COLEMAN is a cofounder of the Community of the Incarnation and the Center for Spiritual Imagination, where she serves as Program Director. She has served the Episcopal Church as healing minister, lay preacher, and adult formation teacher. She lives in Brooklyn with her husband Jeremy and their dog Lilac.

MIRABAI STARR is an award-winning author of creative nonfiction and contemporary translations of sacred literature. She teaches and speaks internationally on contemplative practice and inter-spiritual dialogue. A certified bereavement counselor, Mirabai helps mourners harness the transformational power of loss. She lives with her extended family in the mountains of northern New Mexico.

BRIAN D. MCLAREN is Dean of CAC Faculty and a former evangelical pastor. Championing a more loving, inclusive, and contemplative Christianity, he teaches ways to reconnect with Jesus's message— unconditional love. He is author of *Faith After Doubt* and *The Great Spiritual Migration* and host of CAC's podcast *Learning How to See*.

ALISON MCCRARY is a social justice movement lawyer, spiritual director, and transformative justice practitioner who has lived her life at the intersections of justice and spirituality. A Native Southerner living in New Orleans, Alison serves as the Executive Director at both the School for Contemplative Living and Mission Mycelium. Visit https://www.alisonmccrary.com/.

DREW JACKSON is a poet, speaker, and public theologian. He is author of *God Speaks Through Wombs: Poems on God's Unexpected Coming* and *Touch the Earth: Poems on The Way.* Drew currently serves as the Director of Mission Integration for the CAC and lives in Brooklyn, NY with his wife and daughters.

LEE STAMAN, MLIS, is the library director at the CAC, doing research, acquisitions, cataloguing, and reference work for staff, faculty, students, alumni, and the public. He has a background in theology and philosophy and lives in Seattle, Washington with his family.

Notes

Desert Magic

1   Eucherius of Lyon, "In Praise of the Desert," in *The Lives of the Jura Fathers*, trans. Tim Vivian, Kim Vivian, and Jeffrey Burton Russell (Cistercian, 1999), 210.

2   *The Lives of the Desert Fathers*, trans. Norman Russell (Cistercian, 1981), 73.

3   *The Lives of the Desert Fathers*, 68.

4   Athanasius, *The Life of Antony*, trans. Robert C. Gregg (Paulist, 1980), 68.

5   All stories recounted in this and the next section are from the chapter on "Love" in *The Book of the Elders: Sayings of the Desert Fathers. The Systematic Collection*, trans. John Wortley (Liturgical Press, 2012), 300–309.

6   Columba Stewart, "The Desert Fathers on Radical Self-Honesty," *Vox Benedicta* 8, no. 1 (1991): 7–53.

7   *The Book of the Elders*, 301.

Contemplation Is the Marrow

1   Bede Griffiths, "Feast of St. Benedict," Homily, July 11, 1992, http://www.bedegriffiths.com/wp-content/uploads/2016/05/Feast-of-St.-Benedict.pdf.

1   Barbara A. Holmes, *Joy Unspeakable: Contemplative Practices of the Black Church*, 2ⁿᵈ ed. (Fortress, 2017). See also Barbara A. Holmes, *Crisis Contemplation: Healing the Wounded Village* (CAC Publishing, 2021).

2   The term "Black church" is highly contested. I use the term "Black church" to refer to "those churches whose life and cultural sensibilities have reflected, historically and traditionally, a connection to the larger African American community." This includes historically Black denominations and movements, Black communities in predominantly White denominations, Black independent churches, and multiethnic churches whose "leadership and cultural identity is African American in nature." See Stacey Floyd-Thomas et al., *Black Church Studies: An Introduction* (Abingdon, 2007), xxiii–xxiv.

3   For a more thorough exploration of Black contemplative preaching, see E. Trey Clark, *Black Contemplative Preaching: A Hidden History of Prayer, Proclamation, and Prophetic Witness* (Baylor University Press, 2024). In the book, I delineate three distinctives of Black contemplative preaching: a habitus or disposition of prayer, a mystical hermeneutic, and a meditative homiletical style. I do not have space to develop these here.

4   Though I realize the term Black can be used to refer to people throughout the African diaspora, I am using Black and African American interchangeably in this essay.

5   See E. Trey Clark, "Contemplative Preaching" in *The Oxford Handbook of Christian Homiletics*, ed. Carolyn J. Sharp (Oxford University Press, forthcoming) and Clark, *Black Contemplative Preaching*, chapter one.

6   Part of what follows on Sojourner Truth has been adapted from Edgar Trey Clark III, "Contemplation, Proclamation, and Social Transformation: Reclaiming the Homiletical Theology of Black Contemplative Preaching" (PhD diss., Fuller Theological Seminary, 2021), 68–70. Also, I draw some of the following bibliographic material from Martha Simmons and Frank A. Thomas, *Preaching with Sacred Fire: An Anthology of African American Sermons, 1750 to the Present* (W.W. Norton, 2010), 217–18; and Joy R. Bostic, *African American Female*

Mysticism: Nineteenth-Century Religious Activism (Palgrave Macmillan, 2013), 71–93. See also Sojourner Truth, *Narrative of Sojourner Truth* (Prestwick House, 2007). Since Truth was unable to read or write, her narrative was written by Olive Gilbert. For a major biography of Truth, see Nell Irvin Painter, *Sojourner Truth: A Life, A Symbol* (W.W. Norton, 1996).

7   Truth, *Narrative of Sojourner Truth*, 58.

8   Bostic, *African American Female Mysticism*, 84.

9   Painter, *Sojourner Truth*, 302, Kindle.

10   There are two notable historical reports of Sojourner Truth's speech—one written in 1851 by Marius Robinson and another written in 1863 by Frances Dana Gage. Nell Painter argues that Frances Dana Gage inserted the words "ar'n't I a woman" into Sojourner Truth's mouth when she sent a letter to a newspaper with a modified version of Truth's actual speech. The earlier report of the speech by Robinson did not include the phrase and other embellishments. See Painter, *Sojourner Truth*, chapter eighteen, Kindle.

11   Sojourner Truth, "Ain't I a Woman?" Modern History Sourcebook, Fordham University, accessed 10 June 2025, https://sourcebooks.fordham.edu/mod/sojtruth-woman.asp.

12   Febrianto Febrianto, "Decolonizing Contemplation: Toward a Nonviolent Gaze," *Spiritus* 25, no. 1 (2025): 26–40.

13   Truth, "Ain't I a Woman?"

14   For a more in-depth treatment of Thurman as a contemplative preacher, see Clark, *Black Contemplative Preaching*, chapter two.

15   Howard Thurman, *The Luminous Darkness: A Personal Interpretation of the Anatomy of Segregation and the Ground of Hope* (Friends United, 1965), x.

16   Howard Thurman, *The Search for Common Ground* (Friends United, 1986).

17   Howard Thurman, *With Head and Heart: The Autobiography of Howard Thurman* (Harcourt Brace, 1979), 160.

18   Douglas E. Christie, *The Blue Sapphire of the Mind: Notes for a Contemplative Ecology* (Oxford University Press, 2012), 51.

19   Howard Thurman, "What Shall I Do with My Life? The
     Natural Order," Howard Thurman Virtual Listening Room,
     Howard Gotlieb Archival Research Center, Boston University,
     accessed June 10, 2025, https://digitallibrary.bu.edu/what-
     shall-i-do-my-life-natural-order. Thurman introduces
     the sermon's title as "Jesus and the Natural Order or The
     Great Delusion."

20   Awakenings, 2024, https://www.awakeningsinc.org/.

21   Tia Norman, "When Oppression Pushes Back," message,
     Awakenings, online, April 20, 2025.

22   Howard Thurman, *Jesus and the Disinherited* (Beacon, 1996), 40.

23   Norman, "When Oppression Pushes Back."

24   For an exploration of Amanda Gorman as a contemplative
     preacher, see E. Trey Clark, "Spirit, Spoken Word, and
     the Search for Common Ground: Amanda
     Gorman as Contemplative Preacher," *Homiletic* 49, no.
     2 (2024): 28–41, https://doi.org/10.15695/hmltc.v49i2.5661.

25   Richard Rohr, *The Naked Now: Learning to See as the Mystics
     See* (Crossroad, 2009), 12.

26   Frank A. Thomas, "The Sermon as Essay: James Baldwin as
     Contemplative Preacher," *Homiletic* 49, no. 2 (2024): 82, https://
     doi.org/10.15695/hmltc.v49i2.5667.

27   Thurman, *Search for Common Ground*, 104.

28   I first heard this insight several years ago at a leadership
     conference, and I have slightly adapted it here.

29   Tricia Hersey, *Rest Is Resistance: A Manifesto* (Little, Brown
     Spark, 2022).

Queering the Living Tradition

1   Thomas Merton, *New Seeds of Contemplation* (New Directions,
     1961), 100. *My change from "men" and "man" to "people"
     and "person."

2   Thomas Merton, *Thoughts in Solitude* (Farrar, Straus and
     Giroux, 1956), 79.

3   Thomas Merton: *A Life in Letters: The Essential Collection*
     (HarperCollins, 2008), 22.

4   *A Search for Solitude: The Journals of Thomas Merton*, Volume 3:
     1952–1960 (HarperOne, 1997), 32.

5   The Living School, Trimester 3, Module 8, *Center for Action and Contemplation*.

6   Thomas Merton, *The Seven Storey Mountain*, 50th anniversary ed. (Harcourt Brace, 1998), 462.

7   Merton, *Thoughts in Solitude*, 17.

8   Barbara A. Holmes, *Joy Unspeakable: Contemplative Practices of the Black Church* (Fortress, 2017), 5.

9   Holmes, *Joy Unspeakable*, 26–27.

10   Adapted from Merton, *The Seven Storey Mountain*, 462.

Crisis Contemplation

1   Linda Anderson-Little, "Embracing Darkness and the Solar Eclipse," *SoulStory-Writer*, August 22, 2017, http://www.soulstorywriter.net/109-embracing-darkness-the-solar-eclipse.

2   Shelly P. Harrell, Shena Young, and Thema Bryant-Davis, "African-Centered Cultural Considerations for Contemplative Practices: Mindfulness, Meditation, and Yoga," presentation to the 50th Annual Convention of the Association of Black Psychologists, June 30, 2018, Oakland, CA.

3   This article is adapted from the following sources from Dr. Barbara A. Holmes: "Crisis Contemplation," CONSPIRE Conference (Center for Action and Contemplation, 2018); "Crisis Contemplation," *Living School: Essentials of Engaged Contemplation* (Center for Action and Contemplation, 2024); and selections "The Moan," "The Eclipse," and "Stillness," from Barbara A. Holmes, *Crisis Contemplation: Healing the Wounded Village* (CAC Publications: 2021), 53–57. "Poem Number Two on Bell's Theorem, or The New Physicality of Long Distance Love" from *Directed by Desire*: The Complete Poems of June Jordan, Copper Canyon Press © Christopher D. Meyer, 2007. Reprinted by permission of the Frances Goldin Literary Agency.

Translatio Divina: The Living Tradition of Translating Love into Life Practice

1   Translated from the Coptic by Carmen Acevedo Butcher, word 22 is from my translation of the gospel of toma (Gospel of Thomas) in manuscript form. *True* is linked to *tree* by an

ancient root for "be firm, solid, steadfast; wood, tree," also in *enduring*. As trees make words possible, this trinity of *true, tree, enduring* proves meditation-worthy. We hear anew Howard Thurman saying to his friend Sam Keen: "Follow the grain in your own wood." Be *true* to your deepest roots, word 22 reminds.

2   Translated by Carmen Acevedo Butcher from the Greek in Maxwell E. Johnson, *The Prayers of Saint Sarapion* (St. Vladimir's Seminary Press, 2023), 71, 50. It can also be translated as I do here: "We pray that you make us living people" or "We ask, make us come alive as humans." To be a translator is to see another world and a wealth of possibility in each original text (and person) you meet.

3   Richard Rohr, *Just This* (CAC Publishing, 2017), 15.

4   Carmen Acevedo Butcher, *Practice of the Presence* (Broadleaf, 2022), 54, 87. Br. Lawrence of the Resurrection was born Nicolas Herman (nikɔla ˈer-mὸ). Calm Br. Lawrence and I spent prayerful hours together during the pandemic, from 2020 through 2022. He became my friend Nic.

5   Acevedo Butcher, *Practice of the Presence*, 53, 102, 55.

6   To give a sense of this cloud of witnesses journeying with me, here is a partial list of mystics from whose work I've translated: Angela of Foligno, Catherine of Genoa, Catherine of Siena, Clare of Assisi, Hadewijch, Julian of Norwich, and Marguerite Porete, and others in Carmen Acevedo Butcher, *A Little Daily Wisdom* (Paraclete Press, 2005, 2008); Abbot Ælfric of Eynsham, seventeen Old English homilies on the Gospel of John in Carmen Acevedo Butcher, *God of Mercy* (Mercer University Press, 2006); Benedict of Nursia in Carmen Acevedo Butcher, *Man of Blessing* (Paraclete Press, 2006, 2012); Hildegard of Bingen in Carmen Acevedo Butcher, *St. Hildegard of Bingen, Doctor of the Church* (Paraclete Press, 2007, 2018); desert *ammas'* and *abbas'* recorded sayings and passages in Augustine, Bonaventure, Dionysius, Francis of Assisi, Gregory the Great, Ignatius, Jacob Boehme, John of the Cross, Origen, and Teresa of Avila, plus others in Carmen Acevedo Butcher, *Following Christ* (Paraclete Press, 2010); Anonymous who authored *The Cloud of Unknowing* in Carmen Acevedo Butcher, *The Cloud of Unknowing* with *The Book of Privy Counsel* (Shambhala, 2009, 2018); and Brother Lawrence in Butcher, *Practice of the Presence*.

7 Judith Herman, *Trauma and Recovery* (Basic Books, 2022), 158.

8 Acevedo Butcher, *God of Mercy*, 19, 97–98. Ælfric is pronounced as ˈalˌfrich. In Old English: "gif heo wyrcan nele, nis heo þone lufu." For more information on Ælfric, his life, and the attempts to date it, see Acevedo Butcher, *God of Mercy*, 1–3.

9 bell hooks, *Outlaw Culture* (Routledge Classics, 2006), 59, 298.

10 Jhumpa Lahiri, *Translating Myself and Others* (Princeton University Press, 2022), 58.

11 Lahiri calls translating "the most intense form of reading." Lahiri, *Translating Myself and Others*, 83.

12 Carmen Acevedo Butcher, *The Cloud of Unknowing* (Shambhala, 2018), 83–84.

13 Acevedo Butcher, *The Cloud of Unknowing*, 83–84.

14 Acevedo Butcher, *The Cloud of Unknowing*, 27.

15 Acevedo Butcher, *The Cloud of Unknowing*, 14.

Resting in Darkness

1 John Ruusbroec, *The Complete Ruusbroec*, trans. Guido de Baere and Thom Mertens, vol. 1 (Brepols, 2014), 325.

2 Dante Alighieri, *The Inferno*, trans. John Ciardi (New American Library, 1963), 28.

3 Hadewijch of Antwerp, *Hadewijch: The Complete Works*, trans. Columba Hart (Paulist, 1980), 224.

4 Benedicta Ward, trans, *The Sayings of the Desert Fathers: The Alphabetical Collection* (Cistercian Publications, 1984), 235.

5 W. G. Sebald, *The Rings of Saturn*, trans. Michael Hulse (New Directions, 1998), 173.

6 Pope Francis, "Extraordinary Moment of Prayer Presided Over by Pope Francis: Homily," March 27, 2020, Vatican.va, https://www.vatican.va/content/francesco/en/homilies/2020/documents/papa-francesco_20200327_omelia-epidemia.html.

7 Alejandra Pizarnik, *The Galloping Hour: French Poems*, trans. Patricio Ferrari and Forrest Grander (New Directions, 1998), 27.

8 Julian of Norwich, *Revelations of Divine Love*, trans. Barry Windeatt (Oxford University Press, 2015), 7.

9 Simon J. Ortiz, "Culture and the Universe," in *Out There*

Somewhere (University of Arizona Press, 2022), 104–105.

10   Marguerite Porete, *The Mirror of Simple Souls*, trans. Ellen Babinsky (Paulist, 1993), 91.

11   Thomas Merton, *The Hidden Ground of Love: The Letters of Thomas Merton on Religious Experience and Social Concerns*, ed. William H. Shannon (Farrar, Straus, and Giroux, 1985).

The Integration of Shadow

1   Robert Bly, *A Little Book on the Human Shadow: A Poetic Journey into the Dark Side of the Human Personality, Shadow Work, and the Importance of Confronting Our Hidden Self* (HarperOne, 1998), 18.

Standing at the Threshold: Liminality, Illness, and Transformation

1   Terrill L. Gibson, *The Liminal and the Luminescent: Jungian Reflections on Ensouled Living Amid a Troubled Era* (Wipf and Stock, 2021), 2–3.

2   Gibson, *The Liminal and the Luminescent*, 6.

3   Sharon V. Betcher, *Spirit and the Politics of Disablement* (Augsburg Fortress, 2007), 41.

4   Betcher, *Spirit and the Politics*, 169.

5   Simone Weil, *Gravity and Grace* (Bison Books, 1997), 161.

The Twelve Steps as a Mystical Itinerary

1   Boyd Taylor Coolman, "Spiritual Itineraries," in Edward Howells and Mark A. McIntosh, eds., *The Oxford Handbook of Mystical Theology* (Oxford University Press, 2020), 291.

2   Paraphrase of Bernard of Clairvaux, *On Loving God*, trans. Robert Walton (Cistercian, 1995), chapter 10.

3   *Alcoholics Anonymous*, 4th ed. (Alcoholics Anonymous World Services, 2001), 64.

4   Gregory of Nyssa, *The Life of Moses*, trans. Abraham J. Malherbe and Everett Ferguson, Book II (Paulist, 1978), 131–132.

5   Anna Lembke, in Russ Altman, "The Future of Addiction," *The Future of Everything* podcast, Stanford University

School of Engineering, May 4, 2024, https://podcasts.
apple.com/nz/podcast/the-future-of-addiction/
id1235836821?i=1000651549531.

6 Richard Rohr, *Breathing Under Water: Spirituality and the Twelve Steps* (Franciscan Media, 2021), 3.

7 James Finley, "A Mutual Vulnerability," *Richard Rohr's Daily Meditation*, September 16, 2020, https://cac.org/daily-meditations/a-mutual-vulnerability-2020-09-16/.

8 *Alcoholics Anonymous*, 83–84.

9 Thomas Keating, *Divine Therapy and Addiction: Centering Prayer and the Twelve Steps* (Lantern, 2011), 136.

10 Teresa of Ávila, *The Interior Castle*, trans. E. Allison Peers, (Image Books, 1964), 82.

11 *Alcoholics Anonymous*, Chapter 6.

Engaged Contemplative Christianity as a Living, Life-Giving Tradition

1 These sincere people, I fear, may unintentionally fulfill Jesus's words (in Matthew 16:25) that if we grasp or cling to our life, we lose it, but if we let go, we find life indeed: life to the full, life of the ages. To recall other relevant examples of Jesus's teachings, they unwittingly cling to the wineskins at the expense of the wine (Luke 5:37–39), and they build and preserve tombs to honor the prophets, ignoring the fact that their ancestors in their tradition killed the prophets buried in those tombs (Luke 11:47). In other words, their museums and monuments disguise the sad fact that their tradition never truly understood the prophets they now honor! As Paul boldly put it, their passionate attachment to the "letter" (or details or containers) of their tradition can lead them to choke out the tradition's spirit, content, or primary purpose (2 Corinthians 3:6).

2 We could have a fertile conversation about whether this tradition should be called *engaged contemplative Christianity*, or *engaged Christian contemplation*, or *contemplative Christian activism* ... or something else. In this brief article, I'm leaving those questions for another time and place.

3   This question raises another, related question: How
     might we develop teaching methodologies to help future
     generations enter the tradition as young adults, teenagers,
     or even as children?

4   Questions like these will shape an upcoming series of fall
     events sponsored by the Center for Action and Contemplation.
     Learn more at https://cac.org/.

5   The word *action* may seem clear enough. But in hotly divided
     political times, as soon as you get specific about what kind of
     action you think is important, you find sparks flying. For
     example, is your action aimed at shaming and deporting
     immigrants or defending their human dignity? Is your action
     aimed at reducing fossil fuels for the sake of the planet or
     reducing environmental regulations for the sake of
     the economy?

6   Thankfully, our tradition has more female voices and voices of
     color than many other traditions, but the work of improving
     gender and racial equity also still has a long way to go.

7   We see this problem in the New Testament, when early
     Christians claimed to be "of Paul" or "of Apollos" or "of Christ"
     in a way that created competition and division rather than
     collaboration in the emerging tradition (1 Corinthians 3).

Seven Themes of an Alternative Orthodoxy

1   Adapted from Richard Rohr, with Brie Stoner and Paul
     Swanson, *Another Name for Everything*, podcast, season 4,
     episode 1, May 30, 2020, https://cac.org/podcasts/what-is-the-
     alternative-orthodoxy/.

2   Thomas Aquinas, *De Veritate*, q. 1, a. 8, and *Summa Theologia I–
     II*, q. 109, a. 1, ad 1.

3   Adapted from Richard Rohr, "Good Theology Makes
     Good Politics," CONSPIRE 2021, Center for Action and
     Contemplation, September 2021.

Modern Mystics in the Movements: Incarnating Holy Resistance, Radical Hope, and Contemplative Activism

1   Desmond Tutu, in Deborah Solomon, interview by *The New York Times*, "The Priest," March 4, 2010.

2   David W. Givey, *The Social Thought of Thomas Merton: The Way of Nonviolence and Peace for the Future* (St. Mary's Press, 2009), 38.

3   Ben E. King, Jerry Leiber, and Mike Stoller, "Stand By Me," *Don't Play That Song!* Atlantic/Rhino, 1961.

4   Howard Zinn, "The Optimism of Uncertainty," *Howard Zinn.org* (ZCommunications, September 30, 2004; *The Nation*, September 20, 2004), accessed June 10, 2025.

Recommended Reading

1   Min-Ah Cho, *The Silent God and the Silenced: Mysticism and Contemplation amid Suffering* (Georgetown University Press, 2025), 28.

2   Cho, *The Silent God*, 12.

3   Cho, *The Silent God*, 167.

4   Cho, *The Silent God*, 132.

5   Cho's work can be quite technical at certain points. Here are some texts on silence that may be good places to start before taking on her work:

Haines-Eitzen, Kim. *Sonorous Desert: What Deep Listening Taught Early Christian Monks— and What It Can Teach Us.* Princeton University Press, 2022.

Kenny, Colum. *The Power of Silence: Silent Communication in Daily Life.* London: Karnac, 2018.

Laird, M. S. *A Sunlit Absence: Silence, Awareness, and Contemplation.* New York: Oxford University Press, 2011.

Macculloch, Diarmaid. *Silence: A Christian History.* New York: Penguin Books, 2014.

Maitland, Sara. *A Book of Silence.* Berkeley, Calif: Counterpoint, 2009.

Picard, Max. *The World of Silence.* South Bend, Ind: Gateway, 1952.

Prochnik, George. *In Pursuit of Silence: Listening for Meaning in a World of Noise.* New York: Anchor Books, a division of Random House, Inc., 2011.

Oneing

AN ALTERNATIVE ORTHODOXY

The biannual literary journal of the Center for Action and Contemplation.

Oneing is a limited-issue publication; therefore, some issues are no longer in print. To order available issues of *Oneing*, please visit https://store.cac.org/collections/oneing.

Center *for* Action
and Contemplation

A collision of opposites forms the cross of Christ.
One leads downward preferring the truth of the humble.
The other moves leftward against the grain.
But all are wrapped safely inside a hidden harmony:
One world, God's cosmos, a benevolent universe.